DATE DUE

DEMCO 38-296

THE
NO-SEW
COSTUME BOOK

MICHAELINE BRESNAHAN
AND
JOAN GAESTEL MACFARLANE

The Stephen Greene Press/Pelham Books

THE STEPHEN GREENE PRESS/PELHAM BOOKS

Published by the Penguin Group
Viking Penguin, a division of Penguin Books USA Inc., 375 Hudson Street,
  New York, New York 10014, U.S.A.
Penguin Books Ltd., 27 Wrights Lane, London W8 5TZ, England
Penguin Books Australia Ltd, Ringwood, Victoria, Australia
Penguin Books Canada Ltd, 2801 John Street, Markham, Ontario,
  Canada L3R 1B4
Penguin Books (N.Z.) Ltd, 182–190 Wairau Road, Auckland 10, New Zealand

Penguin Books Ltd, Registered Offices: Harmondsworth, Middlesex, England

First published in 1990 by The Stephen Greene Press/Pelham Books

Distributed by Viking Penguin, a division of Penguin Books USA Inc.

10 9 8 7 6 5 4 3 2 1

Library of Congress Cataloging-in-Publication Data

Bresnahan, Michaeline.
    The no-sew costume book / by Michaeline Bresnahan and
Joan Gaestel Macfarlane.
        p.   cm.
      ISBN 0-8289-0777-3
      1. Costume. 2. Children's clothing.   I. Macfarlane, Joan Gaestel.
      II. Title.
    TT633.B74   1990
    646.4'78—dc20   90-33053
                                                                     CIP

Printed in the United States of America
Designed by Deborah Schneider
Set in Bookman and Kabel by CopyRight
Produced by Unicorn Production Services, Inc.

CONTENTS

With love to Tom, Emily, Charles, Mom, and Dad

—M.B.

With love to Bruce, Andy, Megan, Mom, and Dad

—J.G.M.

ABOUT THIS BOOK

Dressing up is an integral part of life — especially for a kid. Most parents are surprised at how often the need for costumes comes up (more often than they expect!) and how drastically the requirements vary from occasion to occasion. While some costumes are a snap to make, others make you desperate! When confronted with an insistent, out-of-season, offbeat, or short-notice costume request from your kid or kid's teacher, you may find yourself frantically searching the aisles of novelty stores, shocked by the prices, or worse, stranded at the sewing machine at midnight, spending more money and time than a reasonable person should part with. *The No-Sew Costume Book* is here to help you get through these times with ease and style. Featured in the pages to follow is a cleverly thought-out and designed collection of costumes that highlights classic, fun, kid-chic, and clean design and becomes a new dimension in the art of disguise.

Using simple patterns and easy assembly techniques, basic materials are transformed into memorable costumes that you can make without fuss, aggravation, or a lot of talent. If you can cut, glue, and staple, you can do it.

The appeal and wearability of these costumes is virtually ageless, but the needs of children were considered foremost in the designs. Comfort and safety became prerequisites; faces are unmasked and arms and legs free-moving. The costumes can be slipped on and off with ease and can be worn over indoor and outdoor clothing, as needed. They can also be "hand-me-ups," as well as hand-me-downs. Even with all this factored in, you'll find the designs exciting, charming, and amusing. We've tried to give you a wide variety of possibilities (hopefully, we've covered some of those offbeat requests) and to give you costumes with looks that are not only deceptive disguises but deceptively easy to make. We hope you have as much fun with them as we have.

MATERIALS: The materials in this book are for the most part inexpensive and readily available. Although this is a no-sew book, you'll find fabric stores carry a majority of the materials used, including a myriad of great-looking and useful notions, e.g., sequins, wiggle eyes, round-cord elastic, buttons, etc. Craft and hobby stores, as well as variety, hardware, and stationery stores, are also great sources of supplies. The essential pencil, ruler, and scissors are required for every costume and, therefore, have not been included under the "Materials" listing for each costume. Probably your most important tool is a good pair of scissors; they will save you time and aggravation. A fresh bottle of glue can make a difference, too, when a lot of gluing is required; the glue flows more freely, allowing you more accuracy and speed. When working with glue on felt, make a test swatch first—draw a line of glue on a small square of felt and place another felt square on top to secure. On some polyester felts, the glue will seep through the felt, leaving a mark; if this is the case, be especially careful to apply glue in neat lines along the costume edges, so the seep-through pattern does not detract from the costume. Natural-fiber felt does not have this problem. Fabric netting, often used for veils, comes in fine and large mesh, the fine being softer and less stiff. The type of netting (fine or large mesh) is specified under the ''Materials'' listing when it affects the outcome.

MAKING PATTERNS:

All of the headgear designs are uni-sized to fit anyone at any age without any pattern alterations. The body patterns have been sized primarily to fit a wide range of children—with or without an overcoat underneath. Most costumes can be worn successfully by adults without any changes; they just don't cover as much of you! To check the fit, try on or hold up the paper pattern before you lay it out. If you think you'll need extra length, hold off on buying the fabric until you've checked, in case you need a little more. If a costume needs to be lengthened or shortened, in most cases the pattern simply can be cut to the desired length or added to with a piece of paper— you can't go too far wrong. If a special adjustment is needed, it is explained under the ''For Adult Sizing'' section. For mitt patterns, as for the body patterns, hold up to the hand and check for fit, trimming away excess or adding on as necessary.

To make the patterns, you must enlarge the gridded pattern drawings. Most of the costume designs are based on squares, rectangles, and circles, and many of them are symmetrical (both sides the same), making the enlarging process an easy one. In addition, a half-sheet or whole sheet of newspaper (depending on the format) is just about equal in size to a piece of poster board, which makes enlarging some of the simple poster board patterns, such as the heart, star, robot body, and turtle, very easy. You can enlarge drawings using a photocopy machine with enlarging capacities—enlarging to scale—or by using graph paper. To do this, first mark off as many 1-in. grid squares on the graph paper as shown on the artwork (for patterns that are marked 1 square = 2 in., 2½in. grid squares for those marked 1 square = 2½ in., etc. Number the horizontal and vertical rows of squares in the margin on the original; then transfer these numbers to the corresponding rows on your graph paper grid. Begin by finding a square on the graph paper that corresponds to a square on the original. Mark the graph grid with a dot wherever a design line intersects a line on the original. (It helps visually to divide the graph lines into fourths to gauge whether the line cuts the grid line halfway or somewhere to the right or left of it.) Working 1 square at a time, mark each grid line where the design intersects it; then connect the dots, following the contours of the original artwork. It's easiest to draw in the straight lines first, then concentrate on the curves and angles.

CONSTRUCTION TECHNIQUES:

Staples: When working with staples, staple with raw edges away from the body. If not possible, tape the staple ends to prevent ''catching.''

Glue: When making a glue seam, be sure to draw glue in a thin stream, following the edge line. Align and place the piece to be secured directly on top, without shifting, to create a clean seam. When gluing through netting or lace, be sure to use a sufficient amount of glue.

Gathers: Gathers are created by simply bunching the fabric or paper up with the hand to fit.

FINISHING OFF THE LOOK: Since these costumes were designed to be worn over clothes, the clothes you wear should coordinate or blend in with the costume, if possible. Generally, plain clothes are best— turtlenecks or T-shirts and sweatpants or tights. If a storm coat is in order, however, don't fret—the costume will shine through!

ACKNOWLEDGMENTS

The authors' sincerest thanks go to our families and friends for their contributions and generous support throughout this project. Special thanks go to our aunts Joan and Kay for their kind and unfailing support, and to our models, Andy and Megan Macfarlane, Emily and Charles Stanback, Margaret White, Nicole Plumez, Ward Young, Emily Gunther, and Matthew Feldstein.

THE
NO-SEW
COSTUME BOOK

• • • CHAPTER I • • •

MAJOR AND MINOR ANIMALS

PIG

FIGURE A

Here's a blue-ribbon pig—well rounded, fine looking, and fashionably pink. The easy-to-make three-dimensional headband is whimsical and amazingly piglike (see illustration on front cover).

DESCRIPTION: Pig headband, bodysuit, and cloved hoof bands.

MATERIALS: 1 piece of pink poster board; 2 yds. of 72-in.-wide pink felt; 1 square of black felt; 2 large wiggle eyes; double-stick tape; round-cord elastic; small piece of dry household sponge; hole punch; 4 Velcro circles or gripper snaps or 2 buttons.

PREPARATIONS: Enlarge and trace body pattern piece (figure B); headband pieces 1, 2, 3, and 4 (figure C); a 4-×6-in. tail piece; and a 2-×-5½-in. hoof band piece onto newspaper or brown wrapping paper. Extend headband arrows on pattern pieces 1 and 4 an equal amount on each side to a full length of 18 in. for the eye band and 14½ in. for the ear band. Cut pieces out. Following figure B, lay body pattern piece and hoof band piece on folded pink felt; cut out. Trace the headband pieces 1, 2, 3, and 4 and tail piece onto pink poster board; cut out. Measure and cut 4 cloves, 2¾

2

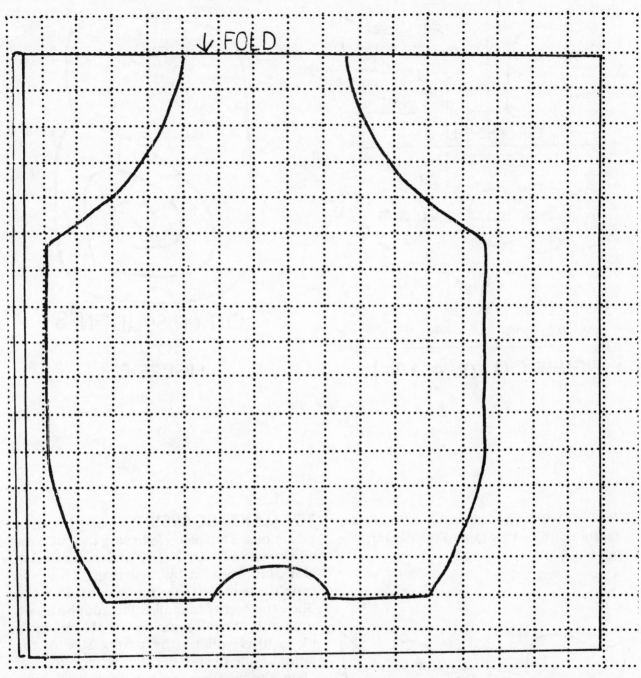

FIGURE B (1 sq. = 2 in.)

× 3¾ in., and 2 nostrils, ½ in. circles, from black felt.

TO MAKE HEADBAND: Glue black felt nostrils onto nose piece as shown in figure C. To create the 3-D effect, pieces are stacked and glued on top of each other. To do this, first glue a ½-in. square of dry sponge onto center circle on piece #2, then glue piece #3 (nose) on top of this; let dry. Using double-stick tape, center and attach the constructed nose segment (pieces 2 and 3 assembled) to piece #1. Glue wiggle eyes as shown in figure D. Punch holes at the ends of the band and tie closed to fit around the head with a piece of round-cord elastic. To attach ear band to headband, measure in and mark 3 in. from the headband ends for placement; secure

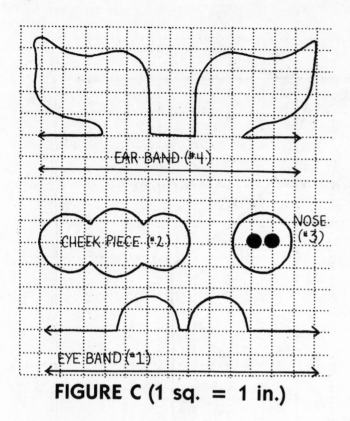

EAR BAND (#4)

CHEEK PIECE (#2)

NOSE (#3)

EYE BAND (#1)

FIGURE C (1 sq. = 1 in.)

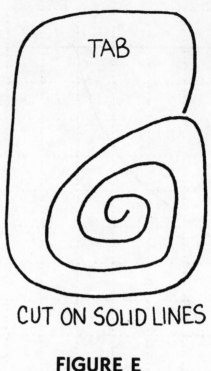

TAB

CUT ON SOLID LINES

FIGURE E

ends of ear bands in place, as shown in figure D, using double-stick tape. Fold ears up for piggy show.

FIGURE D

TO MAKE BODYSUIT: Cut the pink poster board tail piece, following the cut lines, as shown in figure E. Lay bodysuit out flat. Mark tail position by measuring 10 in. up from the center of the crotch; cut a 1-in. slit. Slide the end of the tail coil through the slit until only the tab remains to hold the tail in place (this will be the wrong side of the fabric). Glue the tab in place; let dry. To complete the bodysuit, place front and back together, right sides out. Apply a steady stream of glue ¼ in. from back side edges, align pieces together, and squeeze-press to secure, as shown in figure F; let dry. Pull the tail into a 3-D corkscrew shape. To fasten each shoulder closed for wearing, glue 2 Velcro closures along front and back shoulder edge; let dry. (For gripper snaps, follow same procedure. For buttons, sew button on front and cut a corresponding slit on back shoulder for each side.)

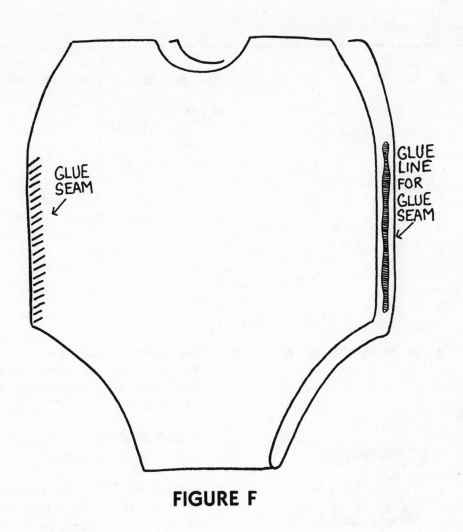

FIGURE F

TO MAKE CLOVED HOOVES: Shape the 4 black felt cloves along the upper lengthwise edges, rounding off the corners (figure G). Glue 2 cloves to each pink felt wristband as shown in figure G; let dry. Punch holes at ends of wristbands and tie closed to fit around the wrist with a piece of round-cord elastic or ribbon.

FOR ADULT SIZING: The bodysuit is the only piece that needs to be adjusted. This can be done easily by adding a minimum of 2 in. to each side and to the length of the bodysuit pattern. Before cutting into felt, hold adjusted pattern up to wearer to assure fit.

SUGGESTIONS: For added fullness, stuff the bodysuit with wadded-up tissue or fabric scraps.

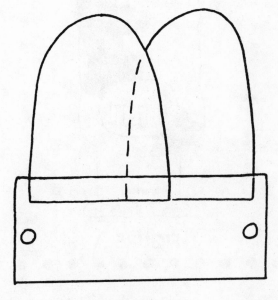

FIGURE G

COW

FIGURE A

Pink-balloon udders add a touch of humor to this classically moo-velous milk machine. The easy-to-make 3-D headband looks like it's right off the farm.

DESCRIPTION: Cow headband and fabric slip-on body with udders.

MATERIALS: 1 piece of white poster board; ½ yd. black, ½ yd. white, and ¼ yd. pink 72-in.-wide felt; black marking pen or black Con-Tact paper in smooth or fuzzy texture; double-stick tape; 4 uninflated, long pink balloons; glue; round-cord elastic; hole punch; dry household sponge.

PREPARATIONS: Enlarge body and tail pattern pieces (figure B) and hat pieces 1, 2, 3, 4, and inner ear (figure C) onto newspaper or brown wrapping paper; extend ear band and nose band arrows an equal amount on both sides for a finished length of 14½ in. for the ear band and 18 in. for the nose band. Cut pieces out. Following figure B, lay body and tail pattern pieces on folded black felt; cut out. Measure and cut a 7-×-10-in. oval from pink felt for the udders. Trace the headband pieces 1, 2, 3, and 4 onto white poster board (figure C); cut out. Cut inner ears from pink felt.

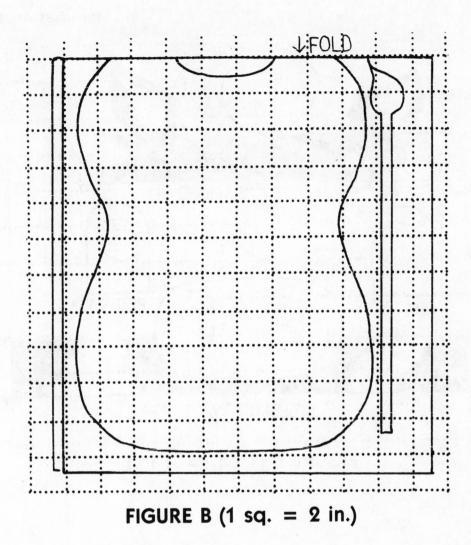

↓FOLD

FIGURE B (1 sq. = 2 in.)

TO MAKE HEADBAND: First apply black coat markings to the nose band and ear band, using the placement in figure C as a guide and black Con-Tact paper (preferably) or an intense black marker. If using Con-Tact paper, trace part of the band edge and then draw an irregular shape using the straight edge as the base. Affix the Con-Tact paper in place on the bands and trim if necessary. Make the eyes by tracing the eye design shown in figure D onto eye pieces 3 and 4. Go over the tracing with a black marker and color in the eye; add black felt eyelids if desired. Using pink felt, cut nostrils (2 narrow 1¾-in. ovals) and 2 inner ears (as shown on earband). Glue or double-stick tape nostrils and inner ears in place (figure A). If desired, outline the nostrils with black marker. To create the 3-D effect, pieces are stacked and glued on top of each other. To do this, first glue a ½-in. piece of dry sponge to the back of the nose at both eye positions as shown in figure E. Glue right side of each eye piece to sponge along the lower edge, making sure that the right eye is on the right and the left eye is on the left and that the eye projection sticks up above the nose section (figures E and F). Let dry. Punch holes at the ends of the band and tie closed to fit around the head with a piece of round-cord elastic. To attach ear band to headband, measure in and mark 4 in. from the headband ends for placement; using double-stick tape, secure ends of ear band in place as shown in figure F. Ears and horn should be along the back edge of the band; fold them up and your cow head is complete.

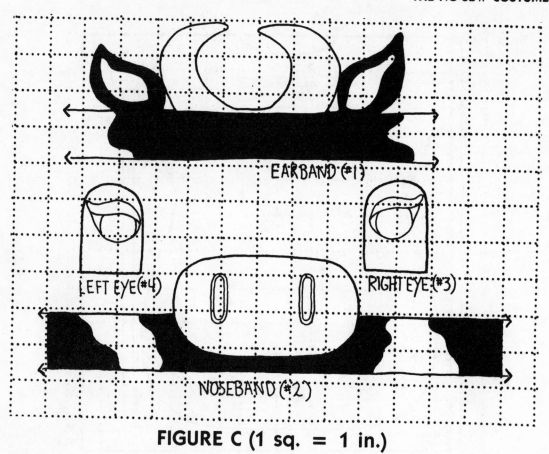

EARBAND (#1)

LEFT EYE (#4)   RIGHT EYE (#3)

NOSEBAND (#2)

FIGURE C (1 sq. = 1 in.)

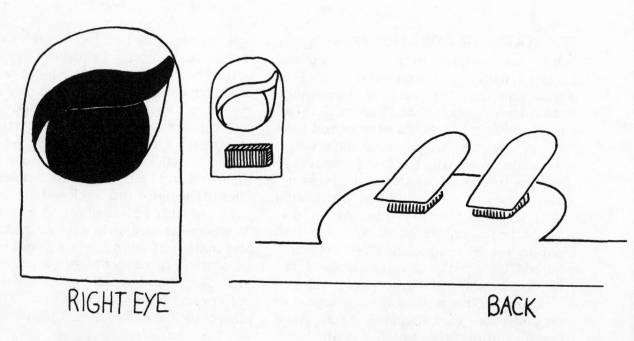

RIGHT EYE   BACK

FIGURE D   **FIGURE E**

BACK INSIDE VIEW
FIGURE F

TO MAKE BODY: Lay body base piece out flat. Cut a 4-in. slit as shown in figure G at center of circle edge (when you wear the slip-on body, the slit will be in the back); try the body on the wearer and extend the slit if necessary to pull it over the head. Cut white felt coat markings (as for headband markings above) and glue to body base as shown in figure G. On the pink felt udder base, make four ¼-in. slashes across the middle. Slide the balloons through the slashes, leaving balloon neck on the back side. Glue the oval onto the body front, positioning and hiding the balloon necks as shown in figure G. On the back, glue the tail in place.

FOR ADULT SIZING: The slip-on body is the only piece that needs to be adjusted. Simply lengthen the body pattern piece.

SUGGESTIONS: A cow bell laced on a ribbon makes a nice addition to this costume.

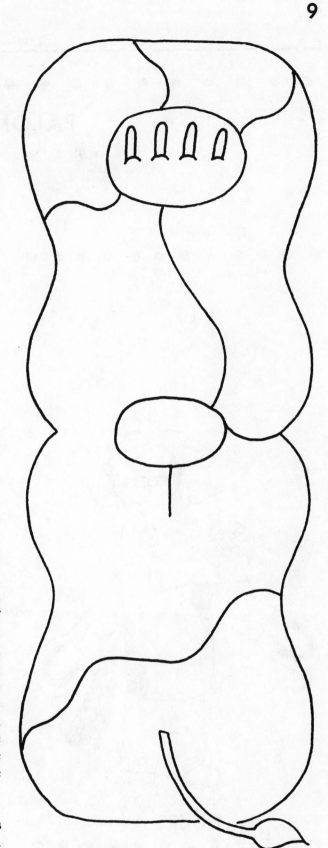

FIGURE G

PALOMINO

• • • • • • • • • • • • • •

FIGURE A

This unique, one-person-horse costume is worn upright for total comfort. The wearer's face is concealed, but vision is unimpaired.

DESCRIPTION: Horse headpiece, slip-on felt body, and hooves.

MATERIALS: 1 piece of white poster board; 1 yd. gray and ½ yd. white 72-in.-wide felt; 1 square each of black and purple felt; glue; hole punch; round-cord elastic; double-stick tape.

PREPARATIONS: Enlarge body, hoof, horseshoe, and tail pieces shown in figure B and head, neck, mane and bangs, eye, pupil and eyelash pieces, nostril, bit, and rein pieces in figure C onto newspaper or brown wrapping paper; cut out. Hold up hoof pattern to the wearer's hand to check fit; if the pattern is more than 1 in. larger than the hand all around, trim to fit. Following figure B, lay body, 2 hooves, 2 tails, and head pattern pieces onto folded gray felt; cut out. Following figure B, lay out neck, mane and bang pieces, horseshoe, tail, eye, and nostril pattern pieces onto folded white felt, placing pieces close together to allow enough remaining fabric to make coat markings for the body; cut out. Trace two base head pattern pieces (figure C) and a 2-×-18-in. band piece onto white poster board; cut out. Lay out and cut bit and rein pattern pieces (figure C) twice from purple felt and pupil, eyelashes, mouth, and nostril pattern pieces twice from black felt.

10

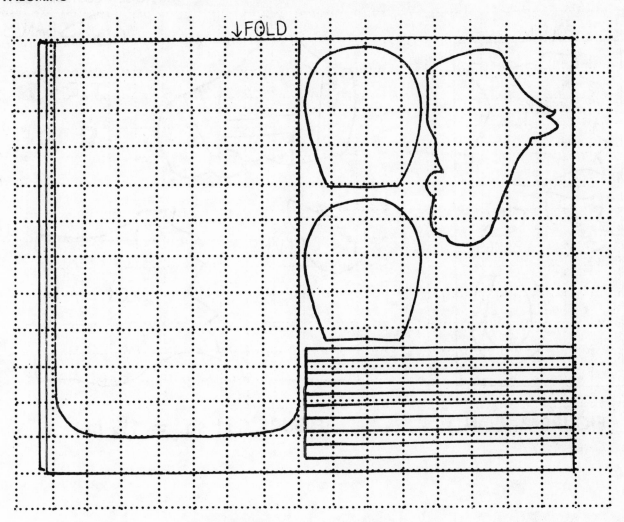

FIGURE B (1 sq. = 2 in.)

TO MAKE HEADPIECE: Cover the base head poster board pieces with gray felt headpieces, making a right and left face (mirror image) as shown in figure D and aligning the edges; glue in place and let dry. To make each eye, layer and glue the eyelash, eye, and pupil together, aligning lower edges. For each nostril, cut white nostril piece slightly smaller all around and glue onto black nostril piece. Position and glue eye, nostril, mouth, bit and rein pieces, and mane and bang pieces onto each headpiece as shown in figure D. For left and right headpieces, glue neck piece onto wrong side of headpiece, positioning it along the lower edge as shown by the dotted line in figure D. The lower edge of the mane will overlap the neck piece slightly. To complete, lay one headpiece, wrong side up, and apply small pieces of double-stick tape from the nose/mouth edge to just past the bit. Place the two headpieces together, right sides out and edges aligned; finger-press to secure together. Fold poster board band in half and place between attached headpieces, positioning as shown in figure E. Using double-stick tape, secure band in place. Punch holes at the ends of the band and tie closed to fit around the head with a piece of round-cord elastic.

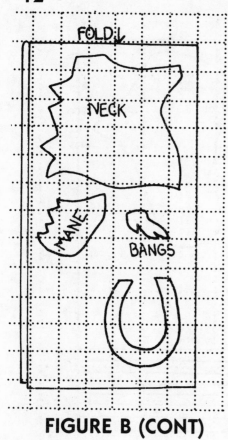

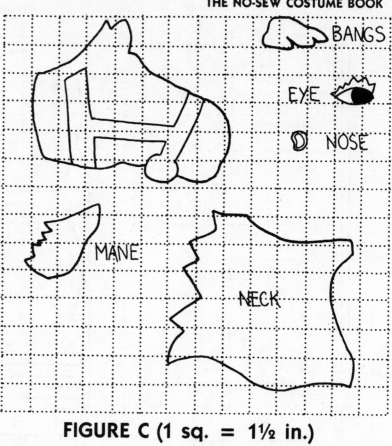

FIGURE B (CONT)

FIGURE C (1 sq. = 1½ in.)

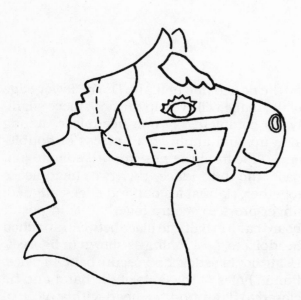

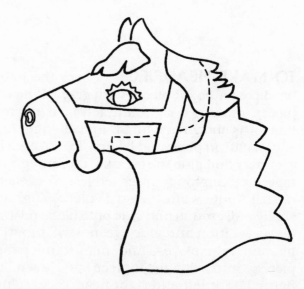

FIGURE D

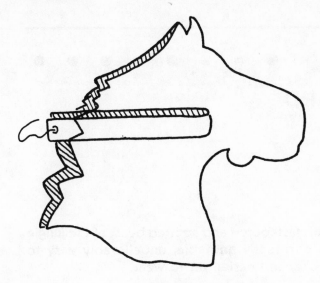

FIGURE E

TO MAKE BODY: Lay body piece out flat. Cut a 4-in. slit as shown in figure F at center of circle edge (when you wear the slip-on body, the slit will be in the back); try the body on the wearer and lengthen the slit if necessary to pull it over the head. Cut white felt coat markings—irregularly cut pieces of felt—as shown in figure F and glue to body base; trim along edges as necessary. On the back, position and glue tail pieces together; cut a small piece of white felt to cover upper tail edges and glue in place as shown in figure F.

TO MAKE HOOVES: For each hoof, place two hoof pieces together. Apply a steady stream of glue ¼ in. from the edge, along the inside (do not glue the wrist edge); align and squeeze-press to secure. Position and glue horseshoe in place as shown in figure A; let dry.

FOR ADULT SIZING: The slip-on body is the only piece that needs to be adjusted. This can easily be done by adding a few inches to the width and lengthening the body pattern piece as desired.

SUGGESTIONS: This great-looking horse can be made in brown, black, tan, or any color you choose, with markings or without.

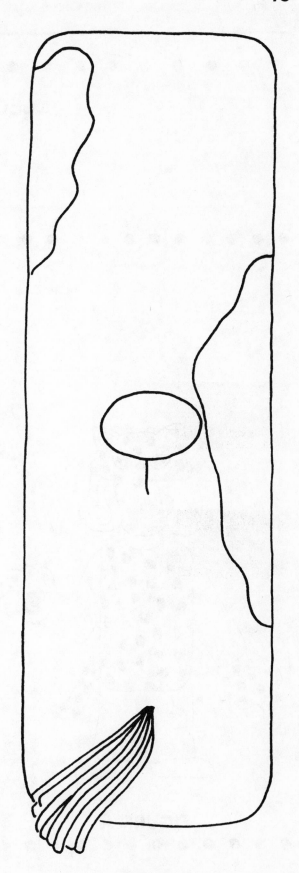

FIGURE F

• • • • • • • • • • • • • • • • • • • •

LEOPARD

• • • • • • • • • • • •

FIGURE A

• • • • • • • • • • • •

This fast-footed and spotted beast of the jungle is purr-fectly adorable, unbelievably easy to make, and easier yet to wear.

DESCRIPTION: Leopard headband, slip-on felt body, and claw paws.

MATERIALS: 1 piece of tan-colored (or yellow) poster board; ¾ yd. of tan (or yellow) and ½ yd. of black 72-in.-wide felt; ⅛ yd. black Con-Tact paper, optional; small piece of white Con-Tact paper or plain white paper; glue; hole punch; round-cord elastic.

PREPARATIONS: Enlarge body, tail, paws, and headband pieces as shown in figures B and C onto newspaper or brown wrapping paper; extend headband arrows an equal amount on both sides to a finished length of 18 in. Cut pieces out. Hold paw pattern up to wearer's hand; if paw is more than 1 in. bigger than hand all around, simply trim away the excess. Following figure B, lay out body, tail, and paws onto folded tan felt; cut out. From black felt, cut 75+ irregularly shaped ¾- to 1-in. spots, ten ¾-in. circular paw pads, two 1-×-2-in. oval paw pads, and 10 skinny 1-in. triangular claws. Trace headband pattern (figure C) onto tan poster board; cut out. From black Con-Tact paper or felt, cut 25 irregularly shaped ½- to ¾-in. spots, a ¾-×-1⅛-in. oval nose, 2 almond-shaped ¾-×-1¼-in. eyes, and 2 triangular 2-×-1½-×-1½-in. ear pieces. From white Con-Tact paper (or plain paper), cut 2 almond-shaped ½-×-⅝-in. pupils for the eyes.

14

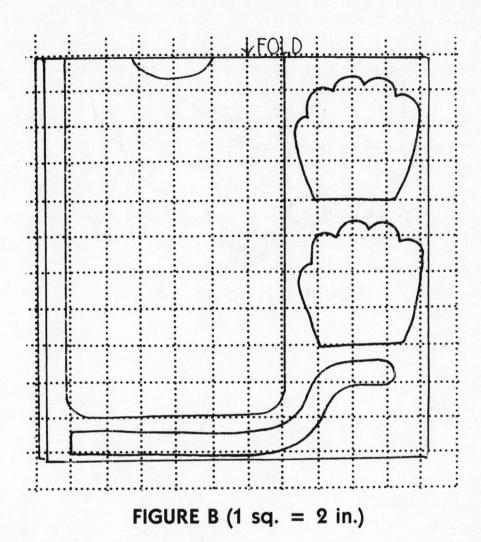

FIGURE B (1 sq. = 2 in.)

TO MAKE HEADBAND: Affix ear pieces, eyes, and pupils (glue on if plain paper) onto the headband as shown in figure C; for nose only, remove half the Con-Tact paper backing, affixing only this much to the headband and leaving the remaining half nose extending below the headband edge. Affix Con-Tact paper spots in a pleasing pattern on the headband (figure C). Punch holes at the ends of the band and tie closed to fit around the head with a piece of round-cord elastic.

TO MAKE PAWS: For each paw, glue 5 felt claws along the scalloped edge, 1 on each scallop (this will be the wrong side). Place a plain paw on top of this, aligning the edges; apply a steady stream of glue ¼ in. from the edges, along the inside (do not glue the wrist edge), and squeeze-press to secure (figure D). To complete each paw, position and glue spots on the paw front and circular and oval paw pads on the paw back as shown in figure D.

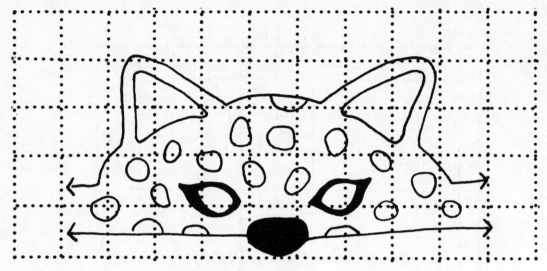

FIGURE C (1 sq. = 1 in.)

FIGURE D

TO MAKE BODY: Lay body piece out flat. Cut a 4-in. slit as shown in figure E at center of circle edge (when you wear the slip-on body, the slit will be in the back); try the body on the wearer and lengthen the slit if necessary to pull it over the head. With body piece laid flat, add the details—spots all over and the tail in the back—and glue in place (figure E).

FOR ADULT SIZING: Simply lengthen and widen the body and paw pattern pieces.

SUGGESTIONS: For a humorous, cartoon look, this costume could be made in hot pink and purple, yellow and red, or whatever you fancy.

FIGURE E

LION

FIGURE A

Making a dramatic, lionesque statement comes easily with this colorful, paper-sculpted mask and slip-on body. Because of the unique hat construction, vision remains unobstructed and unimpaired.

DESCRIPTION: Lion headdress, slip-on felt body, and claw paws.

MATERIALS: 1 piece of yellow or orange poster board; ½ yd. of matching-colored 72-in.-wide felt; ⅛ yd. of black Con-Tact paper and/or a square of black felt; 1 sheet of white crepe paper; 2 large wiggle eyes; double-stick tape; staples; hole punch; round-cord elastic; glue.

PREPARATIONS: Enlarge body, tail, paws, and eye/nose piece as shown in figures B and C onto newspaper or brown wrapping paper; cut out. Hold paw pattern up to wearer's hand; if paw is more than 1 in. bigger than hand all around, simply trim away the excess. Following figure B, lay body, tail, and paw pattern pieces on folded yellow (or orange) felt; cut out. Trace eye/nose piece and a 1¾-×-24-in. mane band onto poster board; cut out. From black felt or Con-Tact paper, cut two 1½-in. circles for eyes and a 2½-×-7-in. rectangle for whiskers. Cut 10 skinny triangular claws from black felt.

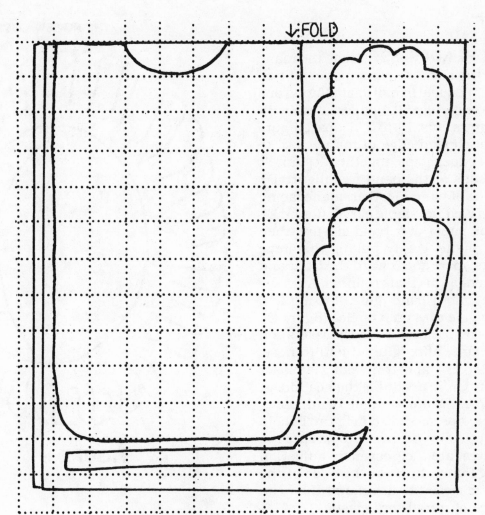

FIGURE B (1 sq. = 2 in.)

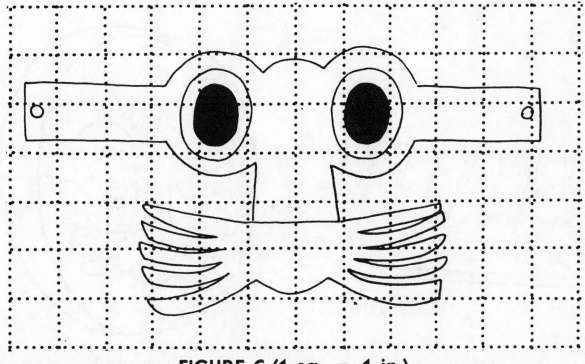

FIGURE C (1 sq. = 1 in.)

TO MAKE HEADDRESS: Make the mane by folding the sheet of crepe paper in half lengthwise; then fold in half again. Along one lengthwise edge, clip all 4 paper layers with 2-in.-deep grass cuts, 1½ to 2 in. apart (figure D). Align unclipped edge of mane close to mane band edge; staple together, leaving ½ in. at the ends of the band free (figure D). Overlap ends of band together, mane facing out, to form a circle; staple closed (figure E). Staple crepe paper over band closure, then "fluff" out mane, gently pulling the crepe paper layers apart and toward the front and back band edges to create fullness. Affix eye circles to eye/nose band (glue, if using felt) and glue wiggle eyes onto circles (figure C). Center whisker piece onto band whiskers and cut nose shape; affix (glue, if felt) to nose/whiskers; let dry and trim along whisker edges (figure C). To assemble the headdress, adhere eye/nose band to mane band, using double-stick tape, as shown in figure F (hold headdress up to wearer's face to be sure the wearer's eyes are not covered; adjust, if necessary). Punch holes at the ends of the band and tie closed to fit around the head with a piece of round-cord elastic.

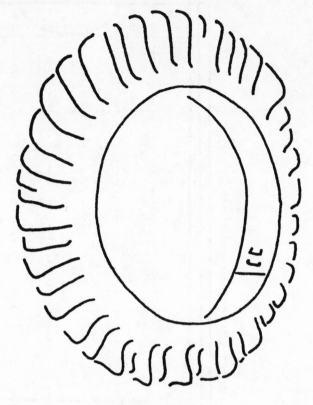

FIGURE E

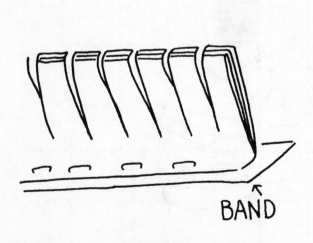

BAND

FIGURE D

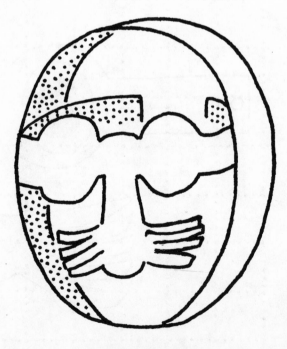

FIGURE F

TO MAKE BODY: Lay body piece out flat. Cut a 4-in. slit as shown in figure G at center of circle edge (when you wear the slip-on body, the slit will be in the back); try the body on the wearer and lengthen the slit if necessary to pull it over the head. Glue tail to back as shown; let dry.

TO MAKE PAWS: For each paw, glue 5 claws along scalloped paw edge (figure H). Place a plain paw on top, aligning the edges. Apply a steady stream of glue ¼ in. from the edges on the inside (but not along the wrist edge); squeeze-press to secure together. Let dry.

FOR ADULT SIZING: Lengthen the mane band piece 2 in. and lengthen (and widen, if desired) the body pattern piece.

SUGGESTIONS: This lion is quite adorable as is, but for an added touch, you could add a medallion of courage.

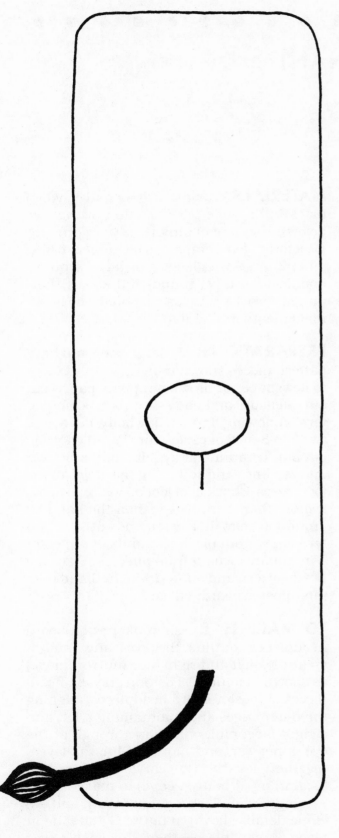

FIGURE G

FIGURE H

ELEPHANT

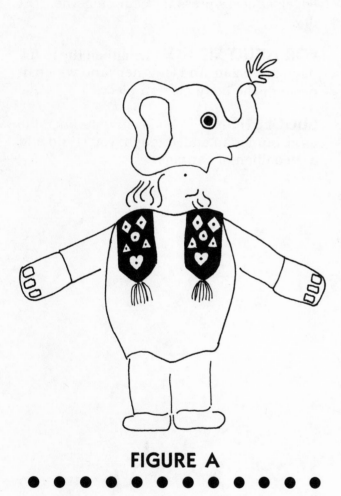

FIGURE A

This jolly elephant is colorfully dressed in circus attire with tasseled sashes hanging from the shoulders and a feather in his trunk. If you like the big look, this one's a winner.

DESCRIPTION: Elephant-head hat, bodysuit with colorful circus sashes, and felt feet.

MATERIALS: 2 yds. of gray and ¼ yd. of black 72-in.-wide felt (for adult sizing, see below); 1 square of pink felt; an assortment of colorful felt scraps, yarns, and/or trims; glue; 2 large wiggle eyes or large sequins; double-stick tape; round-cord elastic; hole punch; two 4+-in. tassels, bought or handmade; feather; 4 Velcro circles..

PREPARATIONS: Enlarge body and head pattern pieces shown in figures B and C onto newspaper or brown wrapping paper; cut out. Measure and cut a 4-×-14-in. sash pattern. Following figure B, lay body, head, and two 5-×-8-in. foot pieces onto folded gray felt; cut out, trimming away felt along inner ear and eye lines and rounding the edges of the foot pieces. Check fit of foot on wearer's hand; if more than 1 in. bigger than the hand all around, trim to fit. Lay out and cut sash pattern twice from black felt, and cut out eight 1-in. square toenails from pink felt. Trace the head pattern and a 2-×-18-in. hatband onto pink poster board; cut out.

TO MAKE HAT: On pink poster board headpieces, outline the eyes and mouth, creating a left and right face (mirror image) as shown in figure C. Position gray felt headpieces on poster board headpieces, aligning the outer edges and maintaining a left and a right face; pink will show through at the eye, inner ear, and mouth. Glue the layers together; let dry. Cut ear along trim line (beginning at bottom edge) to make it free-moving. From black felt, cut mouth and eye circle details shown in figure C and glue in place on headpieces, then glue wiggle eyes

22

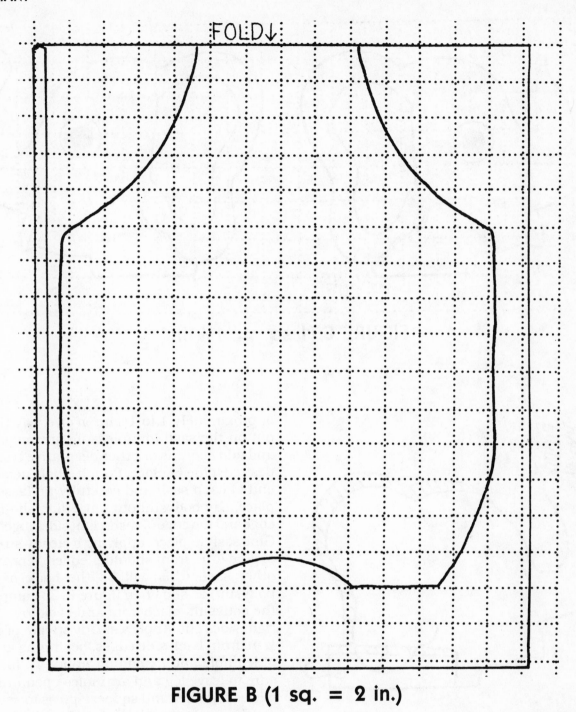

FIGURE B (1 sq. = 2 in.)

or sequins within eye circles. To construct hat, lay one headpiece, wrong side up (pink), and apply small pieces of double-stick tape from the front of the eye, top to bottom, through the trunk, leaving 1 in. untaped at the trunk end. Place the 2 headpieces together, right sides out (gray) and edges aligned; finger-press to secure together. Fold hatband in half and place between attached headpieces, along the lower edge and halfway in, as shown in figure D. Using double-stick tape, secure band in place, making sure not to attach it to the ears. Punch holes at the ends of the band and tie closed to fit around the head with a piece of round-cord elastic.

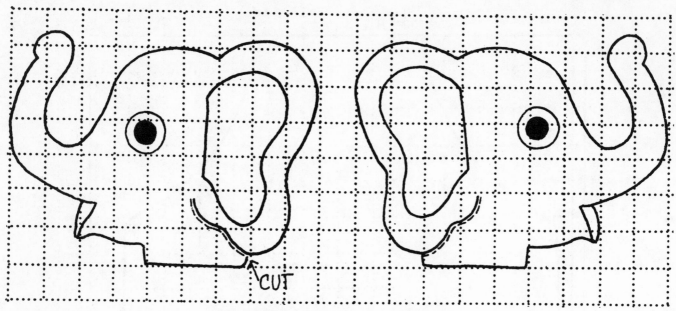

FIGURE C (1 sq. = 1½ in.)

FIGURE D

TO MAKE BODYSUIT: First make the decorative sashes. Using scissors, angle the corners at one end of each sash, forming a V. Cut out an assortment of shapes—hearts, diamonds, squares, triangles, circles—from different colors of felt; the pieces should be approximately 1 to 1½ in. in size. Lay these out on the sash in a pleasing arrangement and add sequins or other decorative trims if desired; glue in place. Punch a hole near the end of each sash and carefully tie tassel in place. Lay bodysuit out flat. Align shoulder edge and top edge of sash, right sides together. Glue sash in place, applying a steady stream of glue ¼ in. from shoulder edges; repeat for other sash (this will be the back of the bodysuit) as shown in figure E. To complete the bodysuit, place front and back together, right sides out. Apply a steady stream of glue ¼ in. from back side edges, beginning at top of leg hole and extending up for 12 in. (Be sure to leave leg and armholes open.) Align pieces together and squeeze-press to secure as shown in figure F; let dry. To fasten shoulder closed for wearing, glue 2 Velcro closures along front and back shoulder edge (on wrong side of back edge); let dry.

TO MAKE FEET: For each foot, place 2 foot pieces together. Apply a steady stream of glue ¼ in. from the edge, along the inside (do not glue wrist edge); align and squeeze-press to secure. Glue 3 or 4 toenails along upper edge (figure A).

FOR ADULT SIZING: The bodysuit is the only thing that needs to be adjusted. This can be done easily by adding a minimum of 2 in. to each side and to the length of the bodysuit pattern. Before cutting into felt, hold adjusted pattern up to wearer to assure fit.

SUGGESTIONS: For a whimsical touch, this elephant can be made in pink all over, or it can take on the look of a storybook character with the addition of appropriate clothes, e.g., vest, tie, king's cape and medallion, etc. For a chubby look, stuff with wadded-up tissue paper or netting.

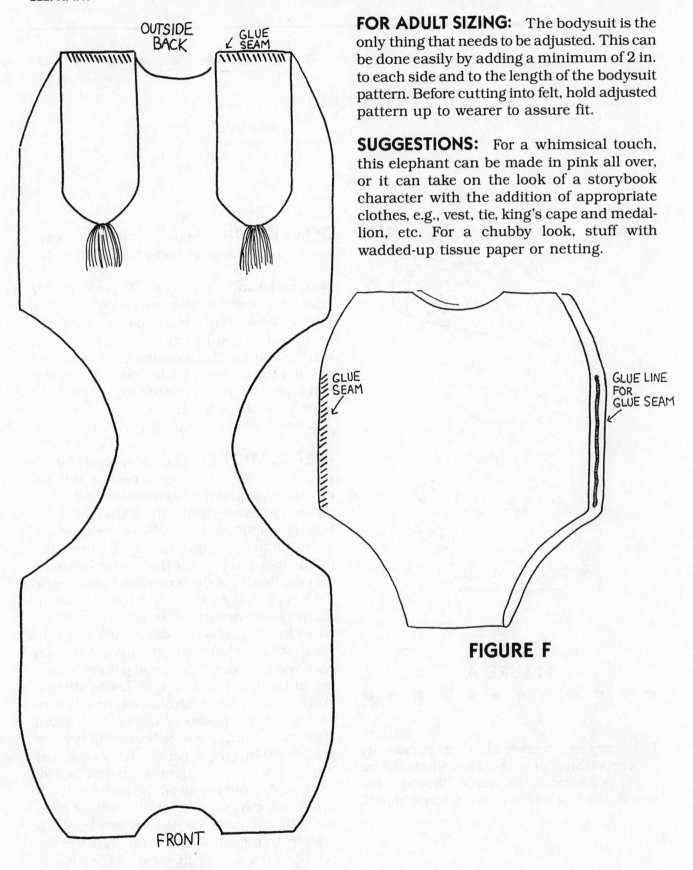

OUTSIDE BACK

GLUE SEAM

GLUE SEAM

GLUE LINE FOR GLUE SEAM

FRONT

FIGURE F

FIGURE E

HIPPO

FIGURE A

This hippy hippo takes on a real personality with accessories of your choice, whether it be a tutu or a necktie. The simple "shoebox" hat evokes the true image of this favored animal.

DESCRIPTION: Sponge-printed hippo-head hat and slip-on body with tutu or tie.

MATERIALS: 6 pieces of pink poster board; black and white poster paints (or gray poster paint); household sponge; 1 square each of black and white felt; round-cord elastic; staples; double-stick tape; adhesive or other thick tape; ½ yd. hot pink netting (for tutu), plus 2 yds. of coordinating-color 1-in.-wide ribbon, or a necktie, plus 2 yds. of coordinating-color 1-in.-wide ribbon.

PREPARATIONS: Lightly sponge-print 4 pieces of pink poster board on one side. To do this, pour and mix some black and white (or gray) poster paint into a shallow, wide bowl or plastic container. Dip one side of the sponge into the paint, then lightly press the paint-coated side onto the poster board to cover with a bit of the pink showing through. Let dry. Enlarge head pattern as shown in figure B onto newspaper or brown wrapping paper (note, this hat is a combination of simple shapes, making pattern enlargement an easy task); cut out. Trace head pattern (marking in the fold lines), 2-×-18-in. headband, and two 2-×-12-in. shoulder bands onto unpainted side of poster board; cut out. From remaining painted poster board, cut twenty-six 2-×-20-in. strips. For the body base, cut 2 rectangles from unpainted poster board, 18 × 22 in., and round off the corners. From black felt, cut two 1-in. circles for the eyes, two ¾-in. circles for the nostrils, two 1¼-×-1¼-×1¾-in. triangular-shaped inner ears (see figure B), and a ⅛-×-12-in. strip for the mouth. Cut 2 teeth, 1 × 1¼ in., from white felt.

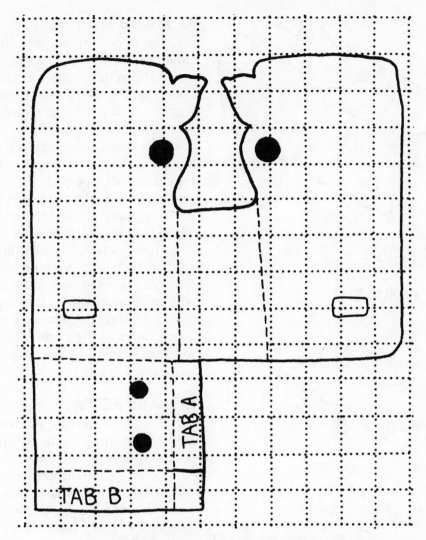

FIGURE B (1 sq. = 1½ in.)

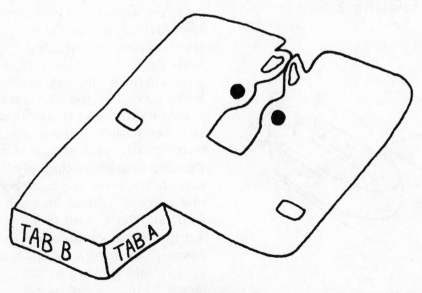

FIGURE C

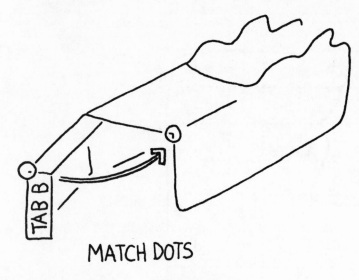

MATCH DOTS

FIGURE D

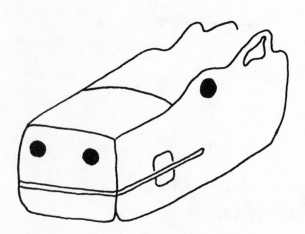

FIGURE E

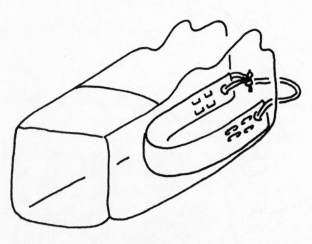

FIGURE F

TO MAKE HAT: Position and glue eyes, nostrils, ears, and teeth onto headpiece as shown in figure B; let dry. Crease the hat along the fold lines (note, there are 5); cut slits along lines A and B, as marked (figure B). Fold Tab A under Tab B (figure C) and Tab B under front face edge (figure D). Staple together at lower front face edge; tape tab down along the inside. Looking in from underneath, the hat resembles an open shoebox. Position and glue felt mouth strip in place, starting on one face, wrapping around the snout, and finishing on the opposite face, as shown in figure E. To complete the hat, fold poster board band in half and position along the inside face sections as shown in figure F. Staple the band to the face on each side, 3 in. and 4 in. from the band end, stapling from the inside. Punch holes at the ends of the band, and tie closed to fit around the head with a piece of round-cord elastic.

TO MAKE BODY: Cover base body pieces with 2-×-20-in. strips, starting from the top and overlapping each preceding strip by approximately ½ in. To secure strips and conceal staples, place unpainted side of strip end under body base, 1 in. in from the side edge; staple in place (figure G). Wrap strip across right side of body base, fold end under, and staple from underneath. Continue in this manner as shown in figure G until the front and back are completed. Hold one body piece up to the wearer and mark the position of the shoulder edges onto the top edge; transfer these marks onto the top edge of the back body piece. Staple the ends of the shoulder bands to the wrong side of the front and back body pieces at the shoulder marks to fit, stapling under the strips, as shown in figure H. Cover staples on the inside, if desired, with long, neatly laid strips of adhesive tape. Punch a hole approximately halfway up both sides of the front and back body pieces; lace one piece of ribbon on each side, through front and back, and tie closed when worn. Tying the pieces together makes the body bow out, creating a fat appearance. To make a tutu, fold netting in half lengthwise and lace a 45-in. piece of round-cord elastic ½ in.

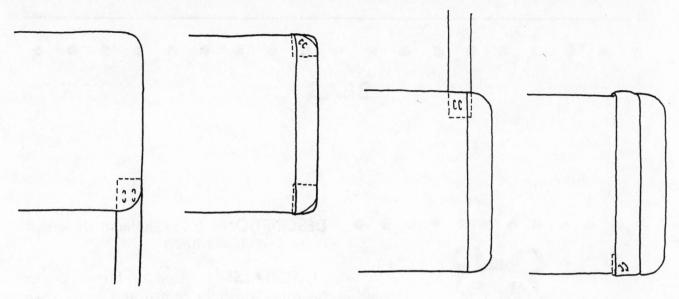

FIGURE G

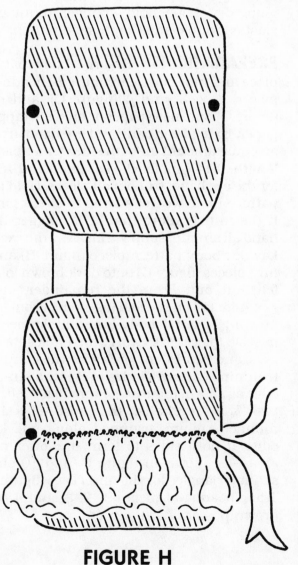

FIGURE H

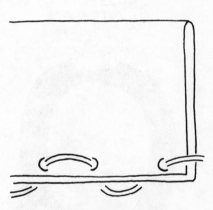

FIGURE I

from the cut edges through both layers, weaving in and out of the holes, every inch or so, as shown in figure I. Repeat this procedure ¼ in. away from first gathering line. Gather the netting up to fit across the width of the body front and tie the remaining elastic ends together on the wrong side. For a masculine effect, simply tie on a necktie.

FOR ADULT SIZING: The slip-on body is the only piece that needs to be adjusted. Simply lengthen body pattern pieces.

SUGGESTIONS: Although the painted body strips add a lot of texture and an appearance of fullness, the front and back body pieces can simply be sponge-painted and the hippo will still be a winner.

BEAR

FIGURE A

Cuddly, comfortable, and cute beyond compare, who could find fault with this adorable bear? The three-dimensional headband, round-bellied body, and claw mitts are all easy to make and are a hit at any age.

DESCRIPTION: Bear headband, slip-on felt body, and claw mitts.

MATERIALS: 1 piece of brown poster board; ⅓ yd. light brown and ½ yd. dark brown 72-in.-wide felt; 1 square black felt; glue; dry household sponge; round-cord elastic; double-stick tape; hole punch.

PREPARATIONS: Enlarge body pattern piece and inner circle in figure B; headband pieces 1, 2, 3, and 4 (figure C); and mitt (figure G) onto newspaper or brown wrapping paper. Extend ear band and eye band arrows an equal amount on both sides for a finished length of 14½ in. for the ear band and 18 in. for the eye band. Cut out all pieces. Hold mitt pattern up to wearer's hand to check for fit. If the mitt is more than 1 in. bigger than hand all around, simply trim away the excess. Lay out body pattern piece (figure B) and 2 mitt pieces (figure G) onto dark brown folded felt; cut out. From the remainder, cut a 4-×-4-in. tail on the fold (figure F). From light brown felt, cut 1 body inner circle piece, 1 muzzle (piece #4), two 1¼-in. circles for the eyes, and two 1½-in. circles for the ear pads, trimming ear-pad circles to create a straight edge as shown (figure C). From black felt, cut two ¾-in. eyeballs, the nose—1-×-1-in. rounded square, trimmed along one long edge at both sides to form the lower nose area—as shown in figure C, and 10 small skinny triangles for the mitt claws (figure G). Trace headband pieces 1, 2, 3, and 4 onto brown poster board; cut out.

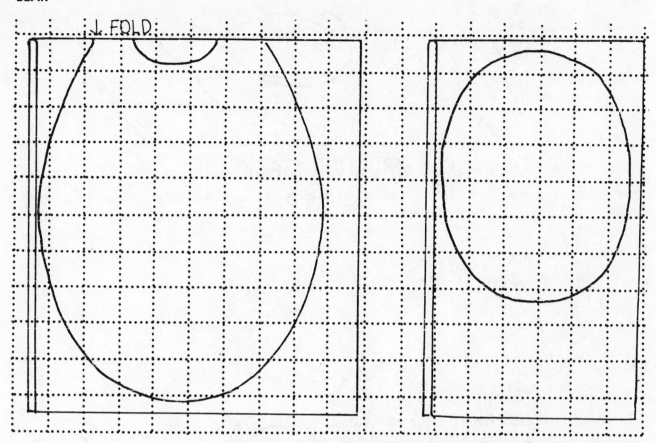

↓ FOLD

FIGURE B (1 sq. = 2 in.)

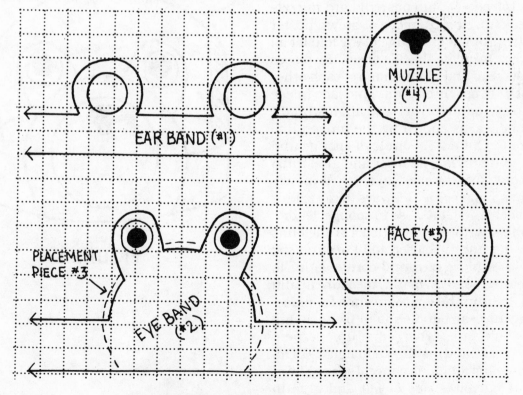

MUZZLE (#4)

EAR BAND (#1)

PLACEMENT PIECE #3

EYE BAND (#2)

FACE (#3)

FIGURE C (1 sq. = 2 in.)

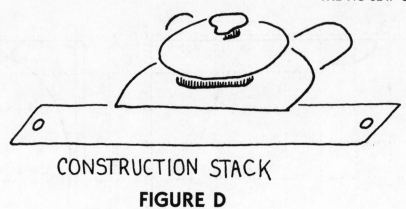

CONSTRUCTION STACK
FIGURE D

TO MAKE HEADBAND: Glue ear pads onto the ears. Glue black felt eyeballs onto brown felt eye circles and position and glue onto eye band as shown in figure C. Glue felt muzzle (piece #4) onto poster board muzzle and black nose onto a piece of brown poster board, trimming to the edge of the felt; let all pieces dry. To create the 3-D effect, the pieces will be stacked and glued on top of each other (figure D). To assemble, first glue face (piece #3) onto eye band; center and align straight bottom edges, as shown by the broken line in figure C. Cut a 2-in. circle of sponge and glue to center of face. Center and glue muzzle (#4) on top of sponge. Cut a ¼-×-¾-in. rectangle of sponge; glue sideways to muzzle at nose placement. Glue nose to sponge; let dry. To finish assembly, punch holes at the ends of the band and tie closed to fit around the head with a piece of round-cord elastic. To attach ear band to eye band, measure in and mark 3 in. from the eye band ends for placement; secure ear band ends in place, using double-stick tape. Fold ears up, perpendicular to ear band, as shown in figure E. Optional finishing touch: To conceal sponge from view, cut narrow strips of felt and glue to sponge edge.

FIGURE E

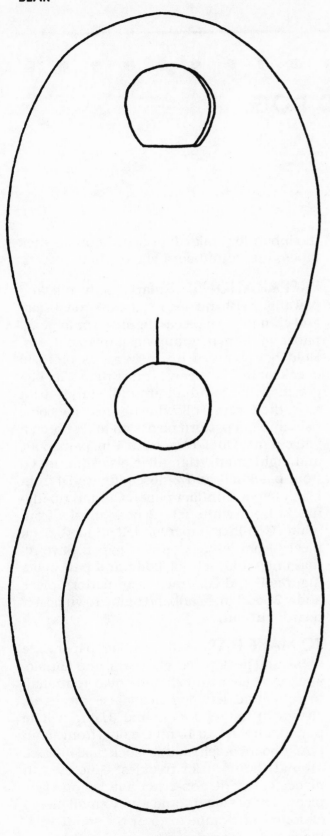

FIGURE F

TO MAKE BODY: Lay body piece out flat. Cut a 4-in. slit as shown in figure F at center of circle edge (when you wear the slip-on body, the slit will be in the back); try the body on the wearer and lengthen the slit if necessary to pull it over the head. Glue felt inner belly piece in center of body front and tail piece on body back (figure F).

TO MAKE CLAW MITTS: For each mitt, place two mitt pieces together. Apply a steady stream of glue ¼ in. from the side edges on the inside (but not along the wrist edge); align pieces together and squeeze-press to secure. Glue black felt claws in place (figure G). Let dry.

FOR ADULT SIZING: The slip-on body is all you need to adjust. Simply lengthen the body pattern piece.

SUGGESTIONS: For a nontraditional teddy bear look, this costume can be made in whatever colors you choose.

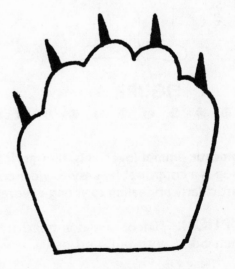

FIGURE G

HOUND DOG

FIGURE A

For a domestic-animal lover, this all-American hound dog is a comfortable, easy-to-wear costume, particularly appealing to young children.

DESCRIPTION: Tricolored dog-head hat, slip-on felt body with tail, and paws.

MATERIALS: 1 piece of brown poster board; ½ yd. brown, ¼ yd. black, and ¼ yd. white 72-in.-wide felt; white (and black, optional) Con-Tact paper; large wiggle eyes; 1½ ft. ribbon for collar (optional); double-stick tape; glue; round-cord elastic; hole punch.

PREPARATIONS: Enlarge body, tail, and paw (figure B) and dog head, nose mask, ear, and chin pattern pieces (figure C) onto newspaper or brown wrapping paper; cut out. Hold paw pattern up to wearer's hand to check for fit. If the paw is more than 1 in. bigger than the hand all around, simply trim away the excess. Following figure B, lay body, paw, and tail pattern pieces on folded brown felt; cut out. Cut 2 ears, eight 1-in. paw spots, and eight small triangular claws (figure G) from black felt and 2 noses (figure D) from black felt or Con-Tact paper. Cut tail tip (figure F) from white felt, 2 nose masks from white Con-Tact paper or felt, and 2 neck pieces from white Con-Tact paper. Save remaining white felt for body and paw spots (figures F and G). Trace head pattern piece and a 2-×-18-in. headband onto brown poster board; cut out.

TO MAKE HAT: Affix Con-Tact paper nose mask and neck piece, glue ears, and double-stick tape nose and ribbon collar (optional) to right and left dog head face pieces as shown in figure D. Optional: Using a hole punch, punch 8 to 10 brown dots from scrap poster board or felt; double-stick tape in place around the nose for freckles. Glue eyes in place; let dry. To construct hat, lay one face piece, wrong side up, and apply small pieces of double-stick tape to cover the snout area. Place the 2 face pieces together, right sides out and edges aligned; finger-press to secure together. Fold poster board headband in half and place between attached face pieces,

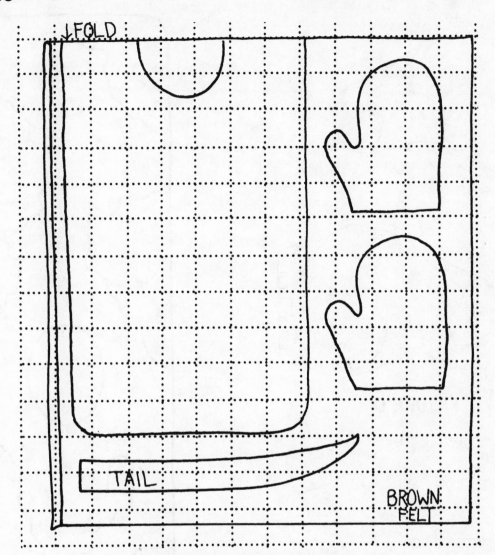

↓FOLD

TAIL

BROWN FELT

FIGURE B (1 sq. = 2 in.)

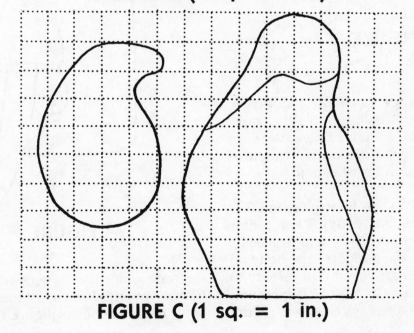

FIGURE C (1 sq. = 1 in.)

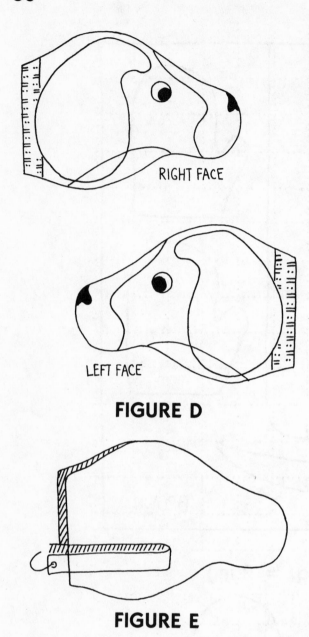

RIGHT FACE

LEFT FACE

FIGURE D

FIGURE E

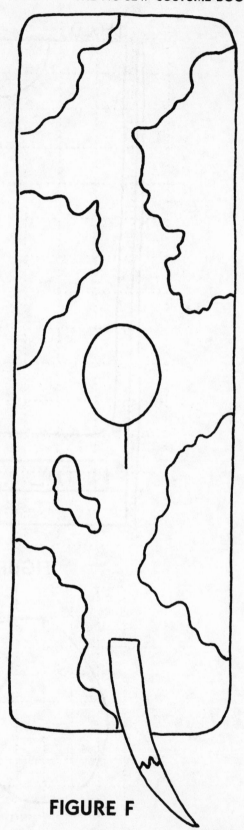

FIGURE F

along the lower edge and about halfway in, as shown in figure E. Using double-stick tape, secure band in place. Punch holes at ends of band and tie closed to fit around the head with a piece of round-cord elastic.

TO MAKE BODY: Lay body piece out flat. Cut a 4-in. slit as shown in figure F at center of circle edge (when you wear the slip-on body, the slit will be in the back); try the body on the wearer and lengthen slit if necessary to pull it over the head. Cut white felt spots and glue to body front and back as shown (figure

F); trim along edges as necessary. Glue white felt tail tip onto brown tail piece; glue tail to body back as shown (figure F); let dry.

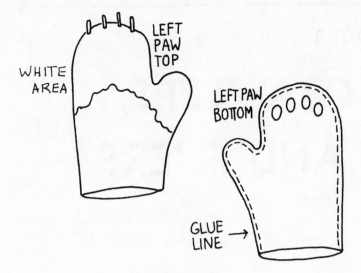

FIGURE G

TO MAKE PAWS: Cut 2 white felt spots equal to the paw width and about ⅓ the length, as shown in figure G; glue in place on a right and left paw piece, trim along edges if necessary, and let dry. For each paw, place a spotted (top) paw piece and plain paw piece together, right sides out. Apply a steady stream of glue ¼ in. from the side edges on the inside (but not along the wrist edge); align the pieces together and squeeze-press to secure; let dry. Glue 4 black paw spots to plain side and 4 claws along white-spotted paw edge as shown (figure G); let dry.

FOR ADULT SIZING: All you need to do is lengthen the body pattern as desired and widen the paws, using your own hand as a guide.

SUGGESTIONS: You can use fun fur for the body, ears, and paws instead of felt, or you can substitute fun fur for the ears only.

CHAPTER II

CREEPERS, CRAWLERS, SWIMMERS, AND FLIERS

OCTOPUS

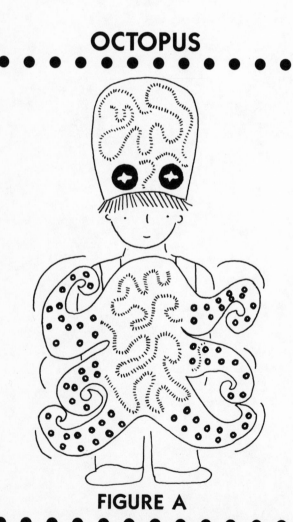

FIGURE A

For all you salty dogs, this whimsical bottom dweller is a real kick! Neon or metallic details give this octopus an electric presence (see illustration on front cover).

DESCRIPTION: Octopus headband and slip-on octopus body.

MATERIALS: 3 pieces of black poster board; small pieces of fluorescent poster board or metallic paper in assorted colors; small piece of black Con-Tact paper or poster board; small piece of dry household sponge (for eye foundation); round-cord elastic; glue; staples; hole punch.

PREPARATIONS: Enlarge body and head pattern pieces in figures B and C onto newspaper or brown wrapping paper and cut out. Trace 2 body patterns, 1 head pattern, and two 2-×-12-in. shoulder bands onto black poster board. Trace two 3-in.-round eye circles onto 1 color of fluorescent poster board. Cut all pieces out (figures B and C). Trace and cut approximately 75 circles, ranging in size from ½ in. to 1¼ in., from fluorescent poster board or metallic paper for the suckers.

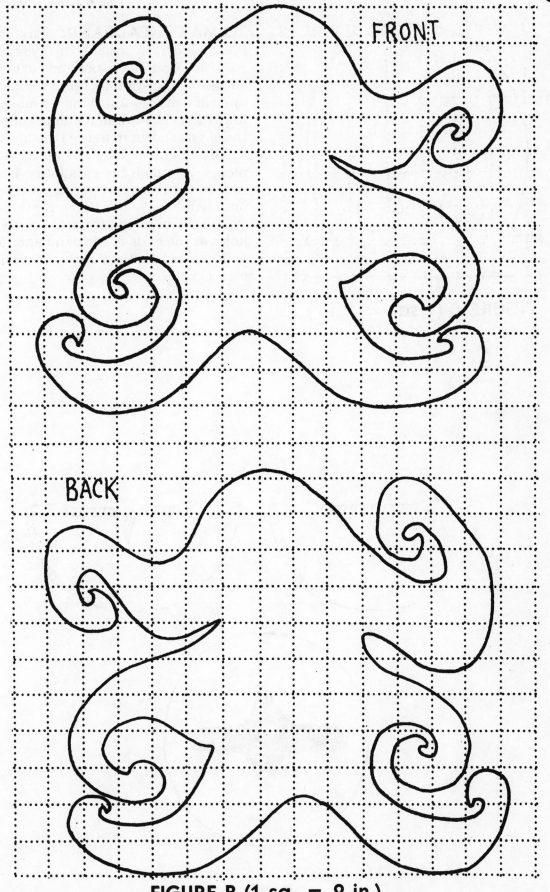

FIGURE B (1 sq. = 2 in.)

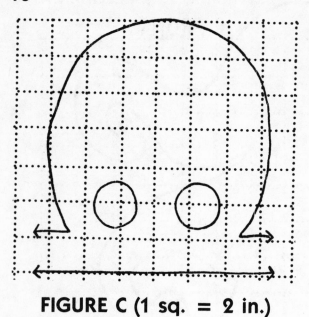

FIGURE C (1 sq. = 2 in.)

TO MAKE HEADBAND: First make the eyes. Trace the 2 poster board eye circles onto the black Con-Tact paper and cut out. One at a time, fold the Con-Tact paper circles in half and cut a narrow 2-in.-long slit along the fold line; then cut a small notch at the center of the slit as shown in figure D. Align and affix the black circles onto the poster board eye pieces. To attach the eyes to the headband, glue two 1-in.-square pieces of dry sponge onto band at eye locations; center and glue eye pieces onto sponge and let dry. Punch holes at the ends of the band and tie closed to fit around the head with a piece of round-cord elastic.

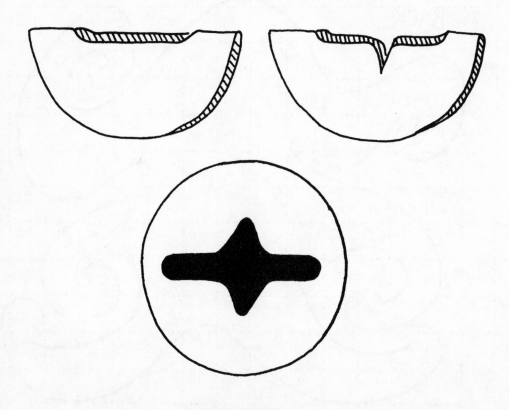

FIGURE D

TO MAKE BODY: On the front body piece, glue circular poster board suckers onto the arms in random fashion as shown in figure E; let dry. Hold this piece up to the wearer and mark the position of the shoulder edges onto the top edge; transfer these marks onto the top edge of the back body piece. Staple the ends of each shoulder strap to the wrong side of the front and back body pieces at the shoulder marks to fit, as shown in figure E.

FOR ADULT SIZING: No changes are necessary.

SUGGESTIONS: This octopus looks terrific made in any fluorescent color.

FIGURE E

LOBSTER

FIGURE A

Slipping into this red-hot lobster with menacing pincer claws, a nicely flanged shell, pop-out eyes, and tentacles is a lot more comforting than a plunge into boiling water! This costume ranks very high on ease of wearability and comfort (see illustration on front cover).

DESCRIPTION: Lobster headband, slip-on fabric shell body, with fins and pincer claws.

MATERIALS: 1 yd. of 72-in.-wide red felt; 1 piece of red poster board; clear Con-Tact paper (optional); 2 large wiggle eyes; round-cord elastic; hole punch; straight pins; ruler or measuring tape; glue.

PREPARATIONS: To maximize the use of the red felt, enlarge body, fin, and claw pattern pieces in figure B onto newspaper or brown wrapping paper; cut out. Following the layout (figure B), pin the patterns onto the folded felt and cut out. Note fin pattern is laid out 3 times for a total of 6 pieces. Enlarge and trace the headband onto red poster board as shown in figure C, extending the band arrows an equal amount on each side to a full band length of 18 in. Affix a piece of clear Con-Tact paper over the tracing to cover the headband (optional) and cut out. The addition of Con-Tact paper makes the headband more durable, but it will survive many wearings without this backing.

TO MAKE HEADBAND: Glue wiggle eyes onto eye projections as shown in figure C; let dry. Punch holes at the ends of the band and tie closed to fit around the head with a piece of round-cord elastic.

TO MAKE BODY: Lay body piece out flat. Cut a 4-in. slit as shown in figure F at center of circle edge (when you wear the slip-on body, the slit will be in the back); try the body on the wearer and extend the slit if necessary to pull it over the head. To make the flanges, following figure D, place pins along both side edges of the front and back shell body. For each side edge, work from the bottom edge up and measure and pin in this sequence: ½

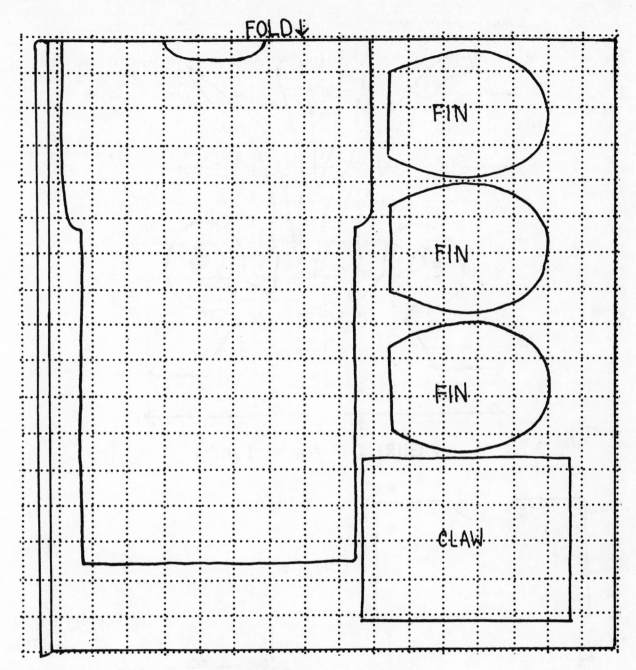

FIGURE B (1 sq. = 2 in.)

in., 3½ in., 4 in., 2¼ in., 4 in., 1¾ in., and 2½ in. You will have 7 pins on each side edge for a total of 28. Working with the shell front first, on each side edge, match up pins as shown in figure E, matching pin 2 to 1, 4 to 3, and 6 to 5; secure with pins. When both front side edges are matched and pinned a fold is created across the shell body. Glue the underside of the fold in place as shown in figure E. Pin #7 marks the hemline; turn up and glue the hem edge in place (figure E). Repeat this same procedure for the shell back. Flip the shell body right side out (the previous folding and gluing created the wrong side), and, using scissors, scallop the edges of the flanges as shown in figure F. Add 3 fins each to the wrong side of the front and back hem edge, angling them as indicated in figure F (center straight and side fins angling outward); glue in place and let dry.

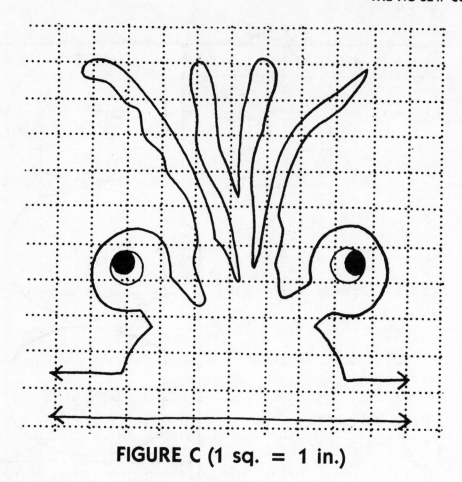

FIGURE C (1 sq. = 1 in.)

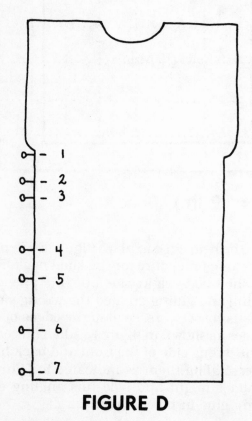

FIGURE D

PLEAT & HEM
CONSTRUCTION

1/2

3/4

5/6

7

FIGURE E

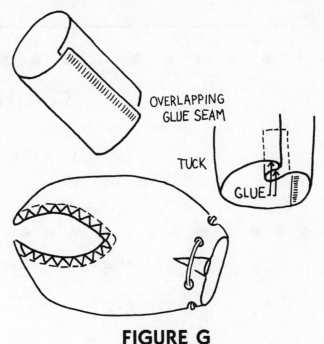

OVERLAPPING GLUE SEAM

TUCK

GLUE

FIGURE G

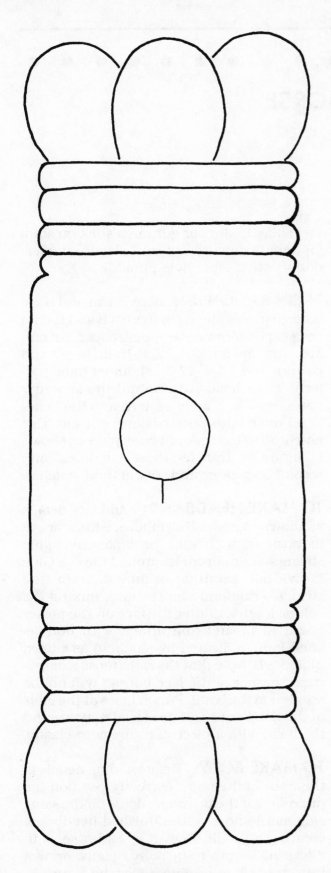

FIGURE F

TO MAKE CLAWS: For each claw, overlap long edge of felt approximately ½ in., forming a tube, and glue in place (figure G). Flatten tube with seamed edge at one side; at opposite side along one top edge, form a ½-in. tuck as shown in figure G and glue tuck in place. Keeping tube in same flattened position, cut claw shape through both layers at untucked edge as shown in finished claw view. Glue these two cut layers together about ½ in. from claw edge; let dry. To form zigzagged edge, pink the claw edge with pinking shears or cut out notches, being careful not to cut into the glue "seam." To finish each claw, using a hole punch, make 4 holes, ½ in. in from wrist end as shown. Lace an 8-in. piece of round-cord elastic through holes, place claw on hand, and tie elastic closed to secure (figure G).

FOR ADULT SIZING: Lengthen the body piece by adding to the top (neck) edge of the pattern—a few inches should be more than sufficient. The claw pattern can easily be lengthened and widened a few inches to accommodate a larger hand.

SUGGESTIONS: Dress this lobster up, if you wish, with a shell necklace or lobster bib or simply carry a shell in your claw.

SEA HORSE

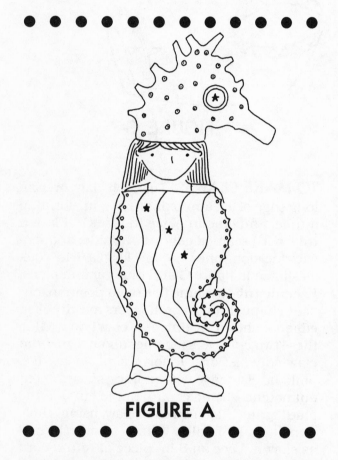

FIGURE A

The ancient-looking, almost mythical sea horse is reinterpreted here for a shimmery look. Simple cutout detailing and decorations make this costume stand out in the crowd.

DESCRIPTION: Sea horse slip-on body and headband.

MATERIALS: 3 pieces of green poster board; 6 yds. of strung sequins (2 yds. per color, preferably hot pink, turquoise, and yellow or green); 4 large pink star sequins or sequin-style plastic stars or gummed stick-on stars (optional); glue; round-cord elastic; staples; double-stick tape; hole punch.

PREPARATIONS: Enlarge head and body pattern pieces shown in figures B and C onto newspaper or brown wrapping paper; cut out. Measure and cut out a 2-×-18-in. headband pattern and a 2-×-12-in. shoulder band pattern. Trace head pattern and the shoulder band twice and body pattern and the headband once onto poster board; cut out. Cut notches around edge of 1 body piece as shown in figure E; transfer these cut lines onto second body piece and cut out these notches.

TO MAKE HEADBAND: Add face details as shown in figure B as follows. Affix star eye in position with glue or tape; then glue strung sequins in circles around the eye. Glue individual sequins—removed from the strings—randomly on the face, mixing the colors; let dry. Center the face on the poster board headband and attach with double-stick tape (indicated by shading) as shown in figure D. Note that the right (nose side) extreme corner of the face bottom will not be secured to the band. Punch holes at the ends of the headband and tie closed to fit around the head with a piece of round-cord elastic.

TO MAKE BODY: Before adding details to the front of the body, correctly position the piece so that the belly/tail edge is on the same side as the nose of the finished headband, creating a profile view of a sea horse as in figure A. To add front body details, draw a thin, wavy line of glue, following figure E,

46

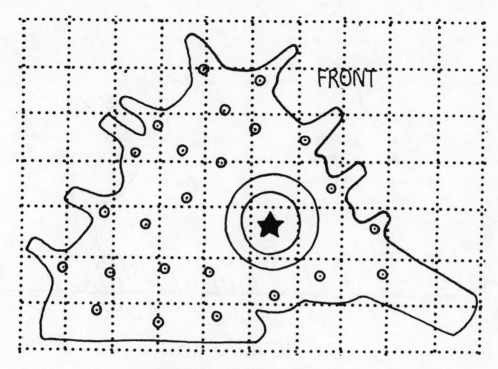

FIGURE B (1 sq. = 1½ in.)

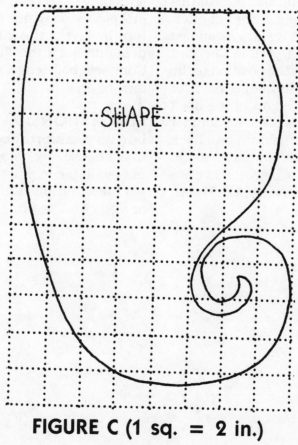

FIGURE C (1 sq. = 2 in.)

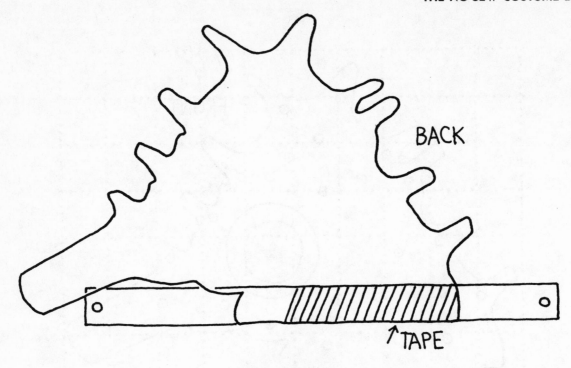

FIGURE D

down the body for the first strand of sequins. Lay the strung sequins, thread side down, carefully in place on the glue line. Repeat this procedure for the remaining 3 lines of alternating sequin colors. Add 3 stars as shown in figure A (optional). Let dry. Hold the front up to the wearer and mark the position of the shoulder edges onto the top edge; transfer these marks onto the top edges of the back body piece. Staple the ends of each shoulder band to the wrong side of the front and back body pieces at the shoulder marks to fit, making sure that the back belly/tail is positioned on the same side as the front as shown in figure E.

FOR ADULT SIZING: To add length to the pattern, draw a line across the body at the level of the star on the right. Cut the pattern in 2 pieces along this line. Create the new pattern by laying the 2 pieces 2 to 4 in. apart, depending on the desired finished length. Complete body edge, repeating the notch pattern freehand.

SUGGESTIONS: Although green seems to be a very seaworthy color for a sea horse, you may choose any color. If strung sequins are not available in your color choices, you can get the same effect using individual sequins or you can use glitter glue.

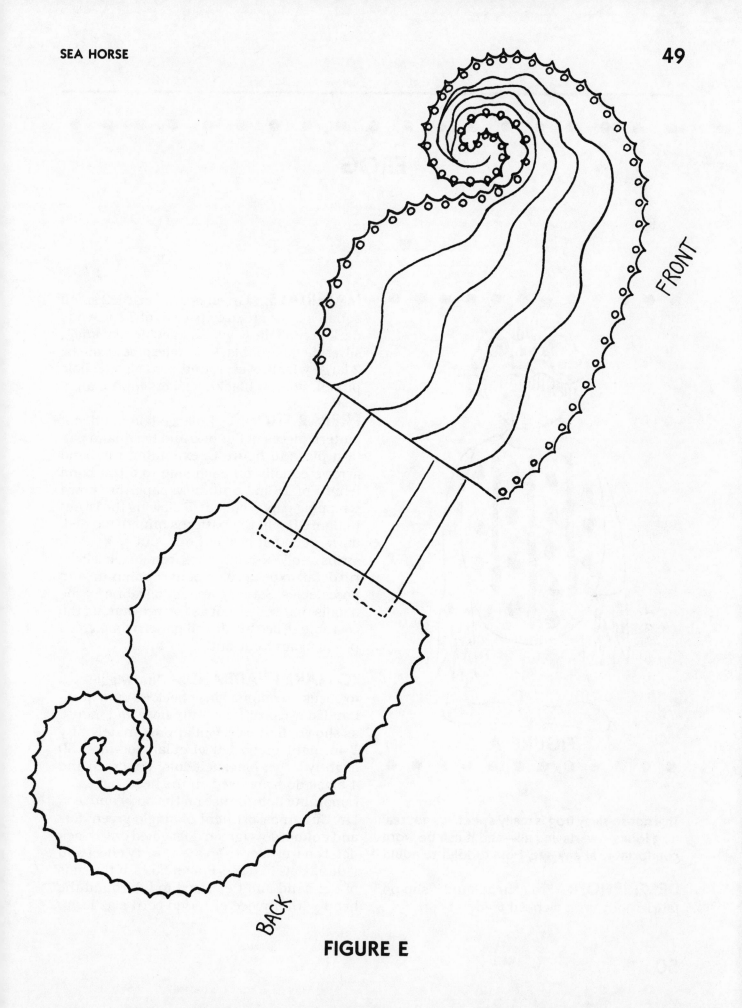

FRONT

BACK

FIGURE E

FROG

FIGURE A

This not-so-slimy frog is really sweet. It's got real frog looks—warts and all—and it can be worn comfortably at any age, from toddler to adult!

DESCRIPTION: Frog headband, slip-on fabric body, and webbed feet.

MATERIALS: Green poster board; 2 small squares light green felt; 1 yd. of 72-in.-wide dark green felt; 1/8 yd. 72-in.-wide black felt; silver-metallic or black-chenille pipe cleaners; 2 large wiggle eyes; round-cord elastic; hole punch; glue; 2 black checkers (optional).

PREPARATIONS: Enlarge body and foot pattern pieces in figure B and headband pattern piece in figure C, extending the band arrows equally on each side to a full band length of 18 in., onto newspaper or brown wrapping paper; cut out. Following the layout in figure B, pin the patterns onto the folded, dark green felt and cut out. Cut 1/2-×-18-in. strips and 1/2-×-5-in. strips from black felt for rib detail to be used on body; cut mouth and nose details. Save the remaining fabric for the details that will be cut as you are making the costume. Trace headband pattern onto green poster board; cut out.

TO MAKE HEADBAND: Glue wiggle eyes to checker centers; glue checkers onto headband at eye positions. Affix nose and mouth as shown (figure C). Cut approximately fifty 1/2-in. light green felt circular dots and 30 slightly larger black felt dots. Ten green and 4 black dots are used on the head; set aside remaining dots for use on the body and feet. Lay out an assortment of single green dots and double dots (green dots glued onto black dots) on frog face to create a warty effect and glue all dots in place. Punch holes at the ends of the band and tie closed to fit around the head with a piece of round-cord elastic.

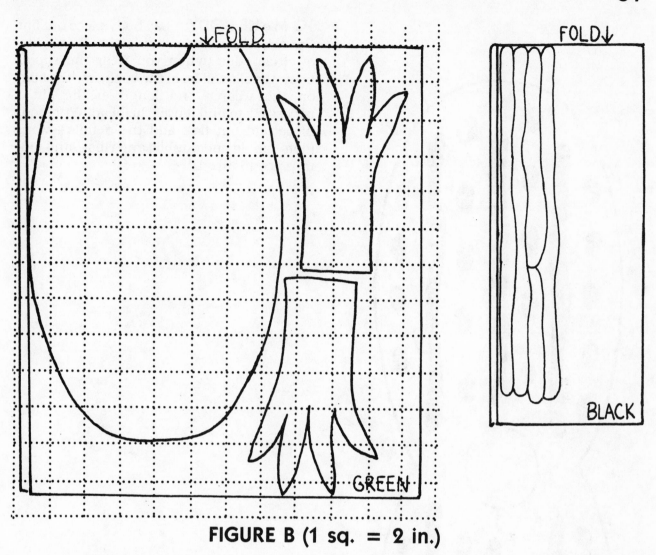

↓FOLD
FOLD↓
GREEN
BLACK

FIGURE B (1 sq. = 2 in.)

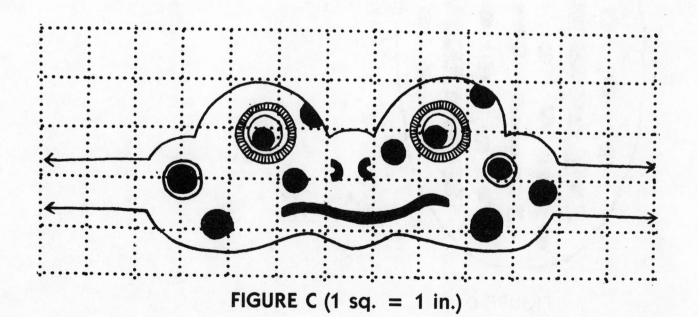

FIGURE C (1 sq. = 1 in.)

TO MAKE BODY: Lay body piece out flat. Cut a 4-in. slit as shown in figure D at center of circle edge (when you wear the slip-on body, the slit will be in the back); try the body on the wearer and lengthen the slit if necessary to pull it over the head. With body piece laid out flat, add the details—warts (dots, single and double) and ribs—and glue in place (figure D).

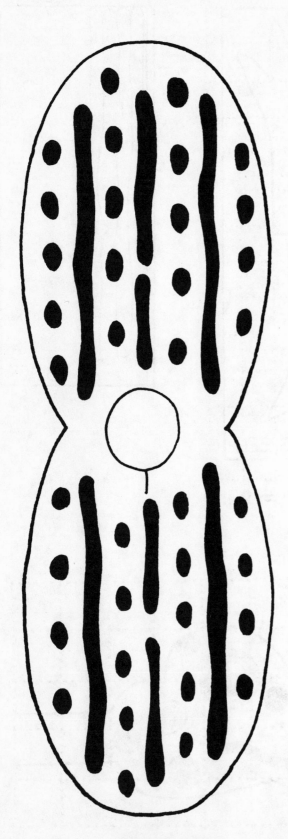

FIGURE D

TO MAKE WEBBED FEET: Lay the 2 foot pieces out flat and position and glue warts in place as desired (figure E). Push (poke) pipe cleaner ends through felt in positions indicated and pinch into a hook to secure in place on wrong side of feet (figure E). Trim ends of pipe cleaners to ¼ in. Punch holes along both side edges and tie with an 8-in. piece of round-cord elastic to form a wristband-type closure (figure E).

FOR ADULT SIZING: The slip-on body is the only piece that needs to be adjusted. This can be done easily by adding a few inches to the width and lengthening the pattern as desired.

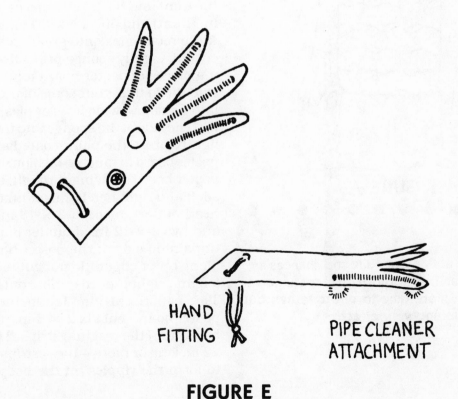

HAND FITTING

PIPE CLEANER ATTACHMENT

FIGURE E

CROCODILE

FIGURE A

You can smile at this crocodile and chances are, he won't bite. The body of this costume requires a little more time to put together, but it's easy to do and very effective.

DESCRIPTION: Crocodile-head hat, sponge-painted (optional) and rippled slip-on body, and slithery hands.

MATERIALS: 5 pieces of green poster board; 3 yds. of green and a small piece of white Con-Tact paper; green acrylic or poster paint and a household sponge (optional); 2 large wiggle eyes; double-stick tape; staples; hole punch; round-cord elastic.

PREPARATIONS: Enlarge head pattern piece shown in figure B onto newspaper or brown wrapping paper; cut out. Measure and cut 2 rectangles from green poster board for the front and back body pieces, one 14 × 22 in. (front) and one 14 × 30 in. (back). Trace these rectangles onto green Con-Tact paper; cut out. Lightly sponge-print all of the remaining pieces of poster board (optional) on one side. To do this, pour some of the green paint into a shallow, wide bowl or plastic container. Dip one side of the sponge into the paint, then lightly press the paint-coated side onto the poster board in random fashion, leaving green poster board showing through; let dry. Trace a left and right head (mirror image) from the head pattern piece, a 2-×-18-in. headband, and two 2-×-12-in. shoulder bands onto the unpainted side of the poster board; cut out along outer edges (do not cut teeth). Trace a left and right mouth outline onto white Con-Tact paper; cut out. Using the remaining poster board, cut six 2-×-8-in. pieces for the hands and the rest into strips, 2 in. wide and 22 in. long or more—these strips will be used to form the ripples on the body.

54

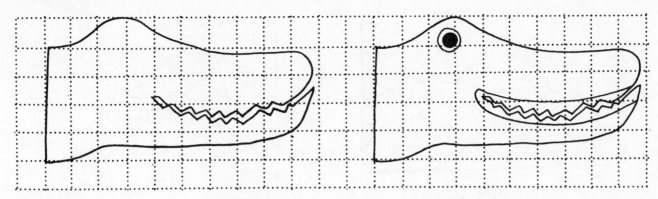

FIGURE B (1 sq. = 1½ in.)

TO MAKE HAT: On painted side of each face piece, affix mouth piece in position; cut upper and lower jagged teeth within the mouth as shown in figure B. The teeth don't need to look perfect, simple triangular cuts will do. Glue eyes in place (figure B). To construct hat, lay one face piece, wrong side up, and apply small pieces of double-stick tape along the entire upper snout. Place the 2 face pieces together, right sides out and edges aligned; finger-press to secure together. Fold poster board headband in half and place between attached face pieces, along lower edge and about halfway in, as shown in figure C. Using double-stick tape, secure band in place. Punch holes at the ends of the band and tie closed to fit around the head with a piece of round-cord elastic.

TO MAKE BODY: First, shape front and back body pieces. For front, simply round off the corners at one 14-in. end of the rectangular front piece; for the back, measure down the sides, lengthwise, and mark off 17 in. At this point, trim each side down to the bottom, forming a tail as shown in figure D, narrowing the width to approximately 4 in. at the bottom. Next, add the textured ripples as follows. Starting with the top back body edge, align and staple one narrow end of a 2-in. precut and sponge-painted strip along side edge. Curve the strip into 4 to 5 waves across the width of the back, stapling in place as you go; staple strip at opposite side edge and trim (figure E). Repeat the procedure of applying the strips in waves to cover the back, aligning strip ends with side edges and butting strips up against each other across the width; staple in as far as possible and then use double-stick tape where necessary to secure waves to body piece. Trim strips along side edges where necessary. Repeat this entire process to cover the body front. To attach front to back, hold the back body piece up to the wearer and mark the position of the shoulder edges onto the top edge of the back piece; transfer these marks onto the top edge of the front. Staple the ends of each shoulder strap, painted side up, to the wrong side of the front and back body pieces at the shoulder marks to fit, as shown in figure D. To finish body and cover staples, align and affix green Con-Tact paper rectangular pieces to wrong side of body front and back; trim along side edges as necessary.

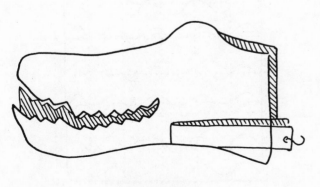

FIGURE C

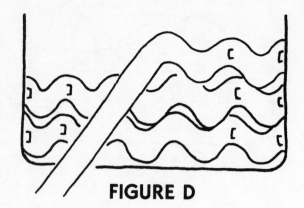

FIGURE D

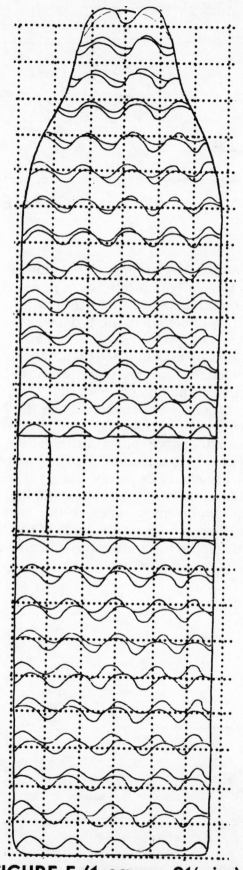

FIGURE E (1 sq. = 2½ in.)

TO MAKE HANDS: Using scissors, taper each 2-×-8-in. hand piece along one end into 2 pointed claws as shown in figure F. For each hand, align and overlap the uncut (wrist) end of 3 pieces; staple together. Punch 2 holes about 1 in. in from side edges and wrist edge, thread an 8-in. piece of round-cord elastic through, and tie to form a wristband closure (figure F).

FOR ADULT SIZING: Widen and lengthen body pieces if desired.

SUGGESTIONS: Although this crocodile is sensational with sponge-printing and ripple strips, it can be made without either or both of these additions and still look terrific (for children under 4, this is probably preferable). Another option is to leave the back plain but jazz up the front.

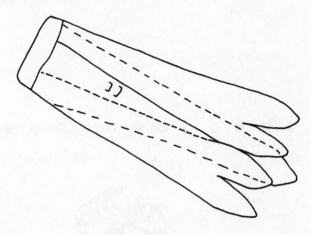

FIGURE F

TURTLE

FIGURE A

This turtle flaunts a showcase house. The stomach evokes the image of a painted turtle, and the 3-D back springs to life. Both effects are created using cutting methods even children can do.

DESCRIPTION: Turtle-head hat and slip-on "box" turtle body (front and back detailed).

MATERIALS: 2 pieces each of black and yellow poster board; 2 yds. yellow and ¼ yd. each of red and black Con-Tact paper; 2 large wiggle eyes; round-cord elastic; double-stick tape; staples; hole punch.

PREPARATIONS: Enlarge head pattern piece shown in figure B onto newspaper or brown wrapping paper; cut out. Measure and cut out a 2-×-18-in. hatband pattern, a 5-in.-square pattern and a 3-×-6-in. rectangular pattern for the back shell details, and a 4-in.-square pattern for the front shell details. Trace head pattern twice, the hatband once onto black posterboard; cut out. Trace the 5-in. square 7 times, and the 3-×-6-in. rectangle twice onto yellow poster board; cut out all pieces. Trace the 4-in. square 6 times and the 5-in. square 4 times onto yellow Con-Tact paper; cut out all pieces. To form the shell body base, fold 1 piece of black poster board in half crosswise; round off the corners to make an oval, approximately 22 × 14 in. (figure C), and cut along the fold to separate the 2 shells. Cut 2 shoulder straps, 2 × 12 in. long, from the remaining poster board.

TO MAKE HAT: Cut a mouth and eye socket for both faces from red Con-Tact paper and affix to right and left face as shown in figure B. Cut neckline scale details, irregularly shaped spots (from yellow Con-Tact paper), and affix to necks following an impression of figure B. Center and tape wiggle eyes in place with double-stick tape. To construct hat, lay one face piece, wrong side up, and apply small pieces of double-stick tape from the back side of the eye socket to the nose, including the

58

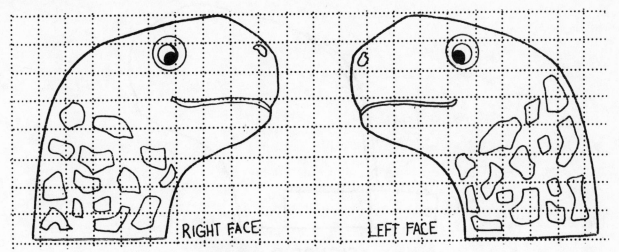

FIGURE B (1 sq. = 1 in.)

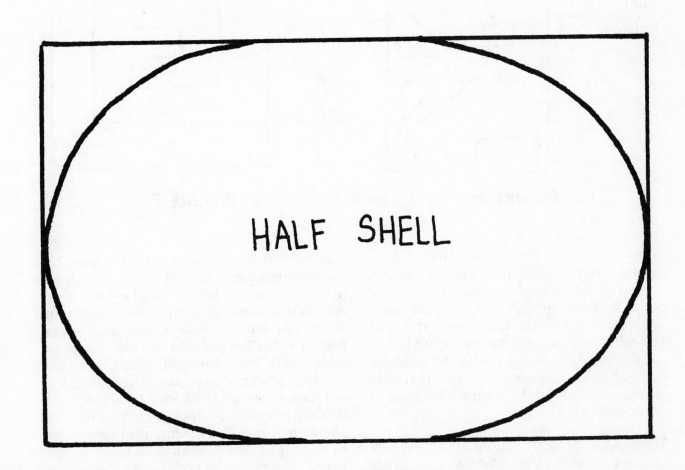

HALF SHELL

FIGURE C

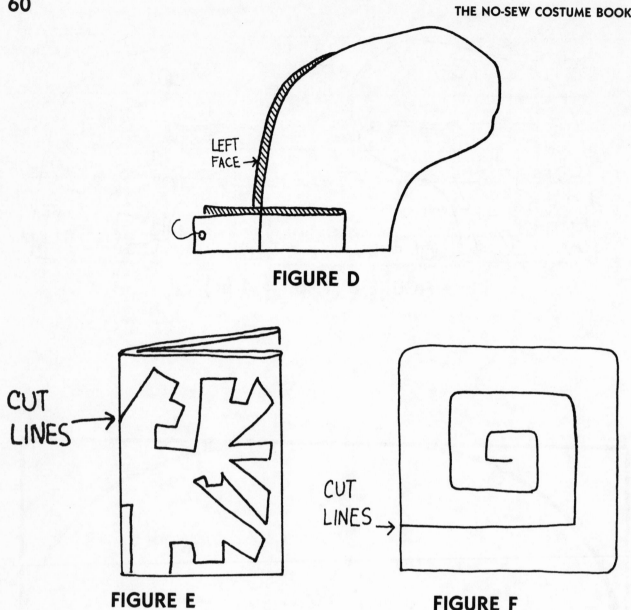

FIGURE D

FIGURE E

FIGURE F

LEFT
FACE

CUT
LINES

CUT
LINES

front neck edge. Place the 2 face pieces together, right sides out and edges aligned; finger-press to secure together. Fold poster board hatband in half and place between attached face pieces, along lower edge and about halfway in, as shown in figure D. Using double-stick tape, secure band in place. Punch holes at the ends of the band and tie closed to fit around the head with a piece of round-cord elastic.

TO MAKE BODY: Round off all corners on detail poster board and Con-Tact paper squares. Beginning with the front shell half, fold each Con-Tact paper square in quarters

and cut into a snowflake pattern (figure E). Following figure G, snowflakes a, b, c, and d are 5-in. rounded squares and e–j are 4-in. rounded squares; affix on shell as shown in figure. Cut and affix small bow-shaped pieces from red Con-Tact paper to decorate the blank edge spaces. For the back shell half, using the rounded poster board squares, cut along the cut lines as shown in figure F to form spirals (springs) in each. Position pieces on shell as shown in figure G, working from the center to the edges; attach with double-stick tape placed along the upper edge of the spiral only, leaving inner cuts free. When pulled from the center, the spirals create three-dimensional springs. Cut small triangles from red Con-Tact paper to decorate outer blank edges of the shell. To attach front shell to back, first hold the front shell up to the wearer and mark the position of the shoulder edges onto the top shell edge; transfer these marks onto the top edge of the back shell. Staple the ends of each shoulder strap to the wrong side of the front and back shells at the shoulder marks to fit, as shown in figure G.

FOR ADULT SIZING: Lengthen and widen the shells by cutting each oval on a separate piece of poster board. Make additional snow-flake squares and springs to fit.

SUGGESTIONS: The colors chosen here create a dramatic, yet realistic, effect, but turtles come in many colors and sizes, so you may choose whatever color suits your fancy. An option for the decorative detailing shown here (snowflakes and springs) is sponge-painting, which would add a colorful, tex-tured effect in very quick time.

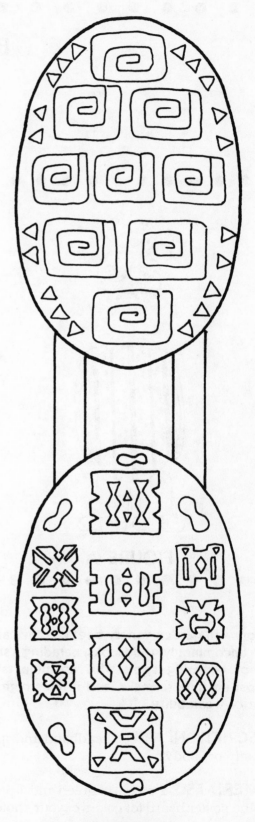

FIGURE G

BEETLE

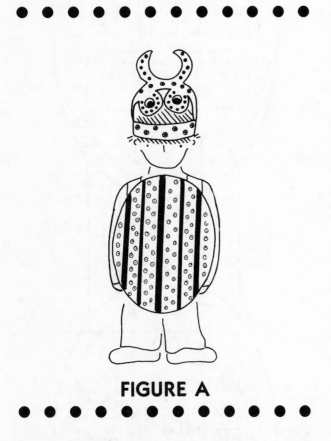

FIGURE A

A common garden-variety beetle comes alive with uncommonly good looks, parading a shell full of glittering spots. This costume takes almost no time to make, and it rates high on ease of wearability.

DESCRIPTION: Beetle headband and spotted slip-on body.

MATERIALS: 2 pieces of green and 1 piece of blue poster board (or colors of your choice);

50+ large sequins; 2 large wiggle eyes; small piece of metallic Con-Tact paper or aluminum foil; double-stick tape; glue; staples; hole punch; round-cord elastic.

PREPARATIONS: Enlarge eye/horn and headband pattern pieces as shown in figure B onto newspaper or brown wrapping paper; extend arrows an equal amount on each side to a finished length of 17¾ in. for the eye/horn band and 18 in. for the headband. Cut out. Trace head pieces and two 2-×-12-in. shoulder bands onto green poster board; cut out. Fold second piece of green poster board in half crosswise; round off the corners to make an oval, approximately 22 × 14 in., and cut along the fold, creating 2 ovals. One oval will be used for the front body piece; cut the other oval in half, lengthwise, to form the wings. Trace the body front onto blue poster board for the body back; cut out. Cut four ¼-×-18-in. front body stripes from remaining blue poster board. Cut two 1½-in. circles for the eyes from Con-Tact paper or foil.

TO MAKE HEADBAND: Position and affix Con-Tact paper eyes (or glue foil eyes) to eye/horn piece as shown in figure B. Arrange sequins on eye/horn and headband pieces in a pleasing arrangement as shown. To attach eye/horn band to headband, measure in and mark 4 in. from both headband ends for placement; using double-stick tape, secure ends of eye/horn band in place as shown in figure C. Horns should be along the back edge of the band; fold the horns up and the eyes down. Punch holes at the ends of the headband and tie closed to fit around the head with a piece of round-cord elastic.

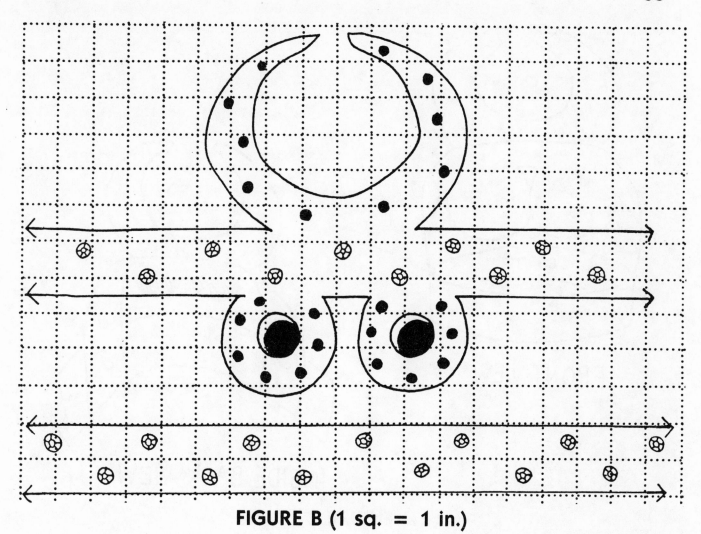

FIGURE B (1 sq. = 1 in.)

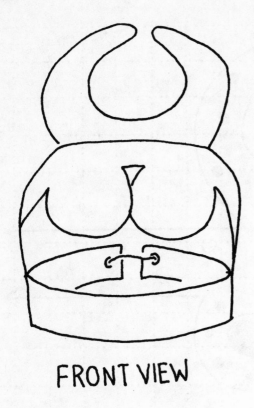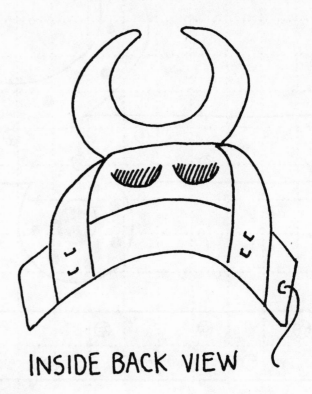

FRONT VIEW

INSIDE BACK VIEW

FIGURE C

TO MAKE BODY: Position and align green poster board wings on top of blue body base; separate the straight, inner wing edges slightly (pushing the wings out a bit) to reveal the blue underbody and secure wings in place at the top, using double-stick tape or staples (figure D). Position and secure sequins on wings in a pleasing fashion, using glue or double-stick tape (figure D). Position and glue blue poster board body stripes on body front as shown in figure D. Add sequins between the stripes as shown in figure D. Hold front body up to wearer and mark the position of the shoulder edges onto the top edge; transfer these marks onto the top edge of the body back. Staple the ends of the shoulder bands to the wrong side of the front and back body pieces at the shoulder marks to fit, as shown in figure D.

FOR ADULT SIZING: Lengthen, if desired, by cutting each oval on a separate piece of poster board, utilizing the full length of the board.

SUGGESTIONS: For a ladybug, use red and black colors. For your own, special, imaginary beetle, use your favorite coordinating colors.

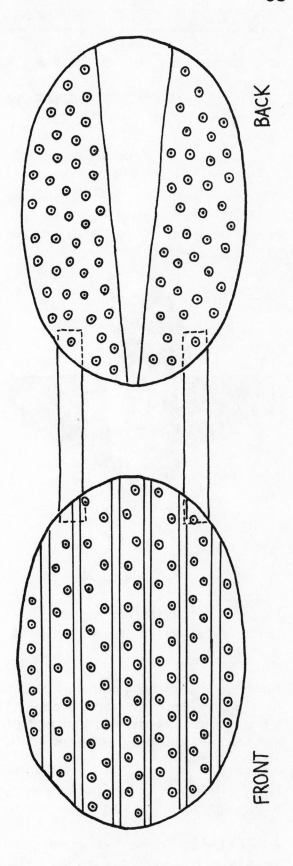

FIGURE D

PREDATORY BIRD

FIGURE A

This generic, high-flying predatory bird takes on a different look and mood, depending on the colors you choose—from menacing (red and black) to patriotic (brown and white) to ethereal (pastels).

DESCRIPTION: Bird headpiece and 2-piece slip-on felt body.

MATERIALS: 1½ yds. black and ⅓ yd. red 72-in.-wide felt; 1 piece of red poster board (or contrasting felt and poster board colors of your choice, substituting lighter color for red and darker for black); small piece of aluminum foil; glue; double-stick tape; hole punch; round-cord elastic.

PREPARATIONS: Enlarge body, wing, shield, wristband, and overbody shown in figure B, and the neck, neck feathers, face, eye pupil, and eyebrow shown in figures C and D onto newspaper or brown wrapping paper; cut out. Following figure B, lay body pattern onto folded black felt; refold remaining black felt as shown and lay out wing (twice), shield, neck, wristband, pupil, and eyebrow patterns; cut out. Lay overbody and neck feathers onto folded red felt as shown; cut out these and fourteen 1½-in. teardrop-shaped feathers. Trace headpiece twice and 2-×-18-in. band once onto red poster board; cut out.

TO MAKE HEADPIECE: Cut 2 eye-base circles from aluminum foil, making them ¼ in. larger than the pupil circles. Glue eye base, pupil, and then eyebrow in position on the poster board face pieces as shown in figure D, creating a left and right face (mirror image). For each face piece, position and glue felt neck-feather piece to face, placing "unfeathered" edge along broken line mark as shown in figure D. Position black felt neck piece on top of feather piece so that cut-feather portion shows; glue in place. Along lower neck edge, glue teardrop-shaped feathers onto scalloped areas; let dry. To construct headpiece, lay one face piece, wrong side up, and apply small pieces of double-stick tape on the beak. Place the two face pieces together, right sides out and edges aligned; finger-press to secure together. Fold poster board band in half and place between attached face pieces, positioning as shown in figure E (broken line marks edge of poster board face piece). Using double-stick tape, secure band in place. Punch holes at the ends of the band and tie closed to fit around the head with a piece of round-cord elastic.

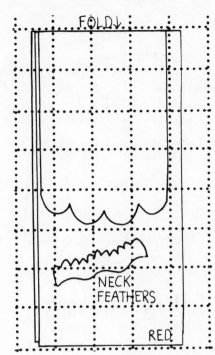

FIGURE B (1 sq. = 3 in.)

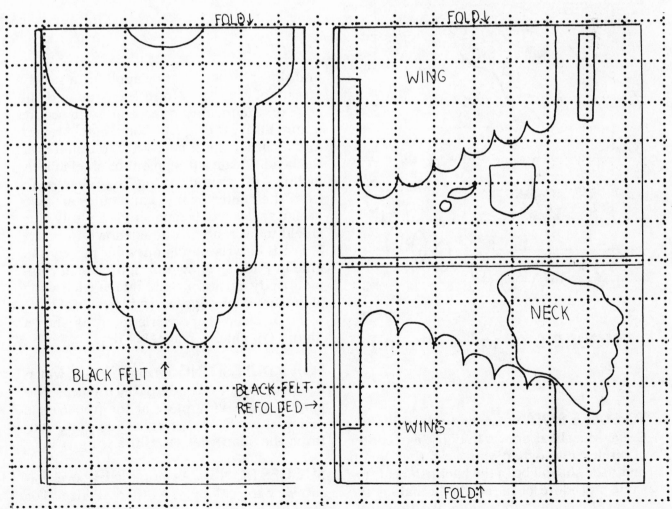

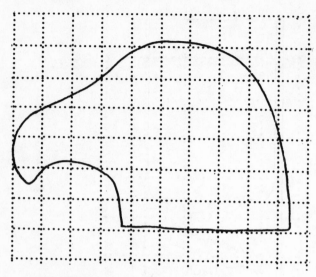

FIGURE C (1 sq. = 1½ in.)

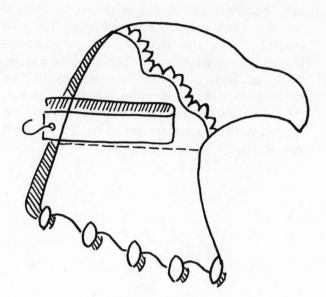

FIGURE E

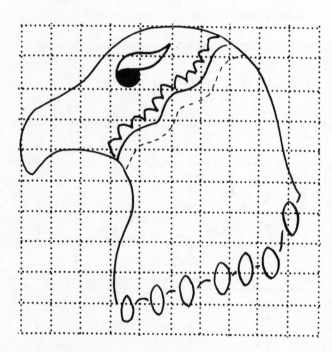

FIGURE D (1 sq. = 1½ in.)

TO MAKE BODY: Lay body piece out flat. Cut a 4-in. slit as shown in figure F at center of circle edge (when you wear the slip-on body, the slit will be in the back). Repeat this same procedure for the overbody, making the slit at the center circle edge. Position overbody onto body base, aligning neck edges

and slits; glue together by applying a steady stream of glue ¼ in. from the neck and slit edge on the inside; squeeze-press to secure (figure F). Try the 2-piece body on the wearer and lengthen slit if necessary to pull it over the head. Create a design on the shield piece, folding it in half and cutting flame shapes out from the center or free-hand-cut your own design as desired. Position and carefully glue shield to overbody front as shown in figure F. Position wristbands on wing pieces and glue at ends as shown in figure G. To complete body, position right side of each wing along upper tab edge onto wrong side of body piece at sleeve cap, overlapping as shown (figure G); glue in place. Let dry.

FOR ADULT SIZING: Lengthen and widen the body and overbody pattern pieces and lengthen the wing piece at the upper edge (below the tab), widening as you go to continue the shape design of the wing.

SUGGESTIONS: As suggested above, you can vary the colors for a different effect. For the shield, you can purchase a decorative badge, instead of making a cutout.

FIGURE F

FIGURE G

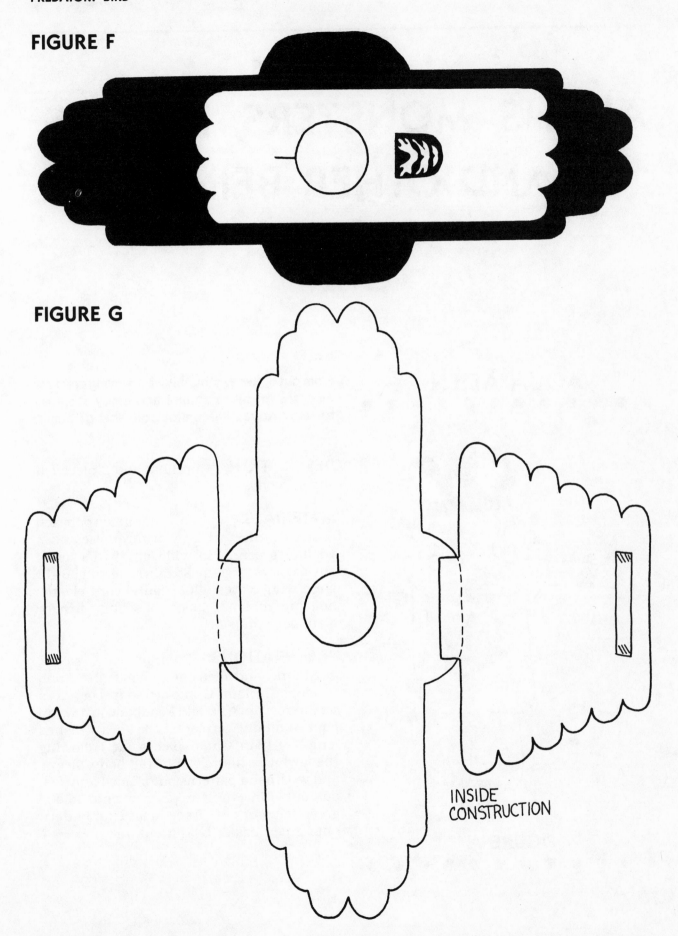

INSIDE
CONSTRUCTION

CHAPTER III

ALIENS, MONSTERS, FAERIES, AND OTHER BEINGS

• • • • • • • • • • • AQUA ALIEN

FIGURE A

• • • • • • • • • • • •

From out of the depths, this water-loving creature emerges for all to admire and enjoy. It's easy to see, "Aqua's" a comfortable sort of being.

DESCRIPTION: Coral hat and 2-piece felt slip-on body.

MATERIALS: 1 piece of lime green or peach poster board; ⅔ yd. gray or turquoise and ½ yd. lime green 72-in.-wide felt; ¼ yd. each of any 4 colors large-mesh fabric netting; 8–10 large wiggle eyes; glue; round-cord elastic; hole punch; small pieces of string, yarn, or 4 rubber bands.

PREPARATIONS: Enlarge body, sleeve, wristband, and alien emblem in figure B and headband in figure C onto newspaper or brown wrapping paper; extend headband arrows an equal amount on each side to a finished length of 18 in. Cut all pieces out. Following the layout in figure B, pin the body, sleeve, and wristband patterns onto folded gray felt; cut out. Pin emblem pattern onto folded green felt; cut out. Trace headband pattern onto green poster board; cut out.

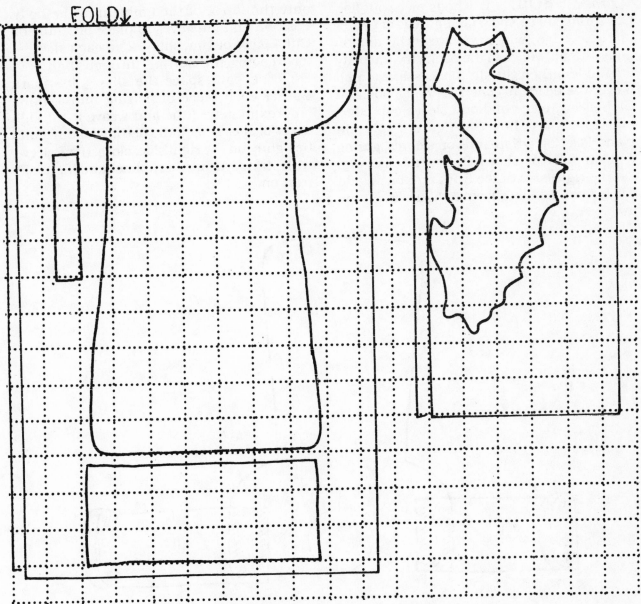

FOLD↓

FIGURE B (1 sq. = 2 in.)

TO MAKE HEADBAND: Glue eyes in place on headband as shown in figure C.

Punch holes at ends of band and tie closed to fit around the head with a piece of round-cord elastic (figure C).

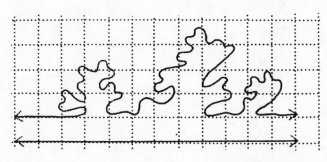 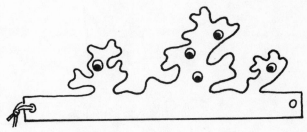

FIGURE C (1 sq. = 2 in.)

TO MAKE BODY: Lay body piece out flat. Cut a 4-in. slit as shown in figure D at center of circle edge (when you wear the slip-on body, the slit will be in the back); try the body on and lengthen the slit if necessary to pull it over the head. To construct body, position each sleeve piece on body sleeve cap edge, overlapping as shown in figure D; glue in place. Position wristbands on sleeves, gluing ends in place as shown in figure D. Let dry. On the right side of the front and back, add the felt emblem as shown in figure E, gluing

only the top ¼ of the emblem to the body. Position and glue eyes in place on emblem. Cut 4 pairs of 1-in. slits—2 on each sleeve—for weaving the netting through (figure E). For each pair, space the slits ½ in. apart. Gather each piece of netting into a 14-in. (approximately) tube and weave it through a pair of slits. Bunch the netting together and tie tightly on the right side, close to the sleeve, with string, yarn, or a rubber band (figure F); trim ends.

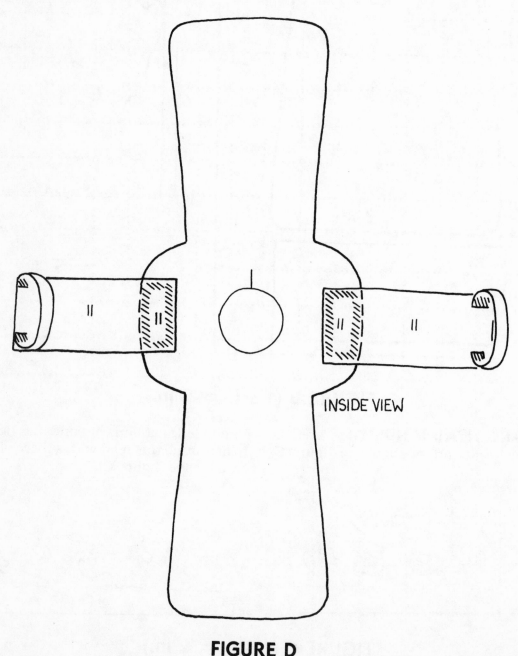

INSIDE VIEW

FIGURE D

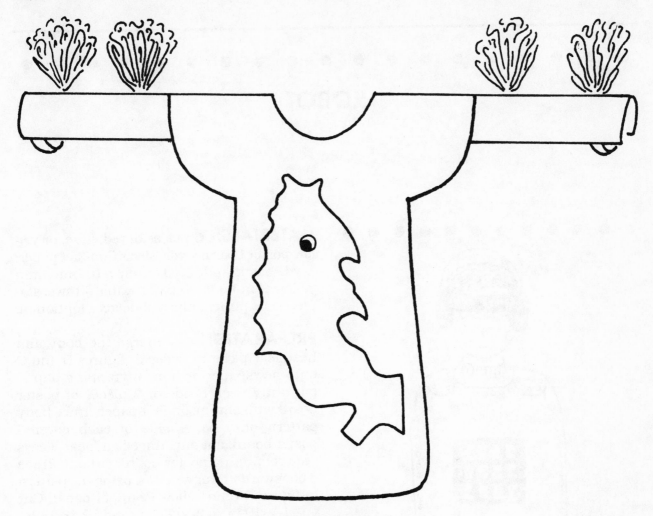

FIGURE E

BUNCH NET

TIE TIGHTLY

FIGURE F

ADULT SIZING: No alterations are necessary, although you may choose to lengthen the body.

SUGGESTIONS: Water colors have been chosen for this alien, although you may choose other colors to your taste. The emblem can be dressed up with the addition of shiny green and blue sequins.

ROBOT

FIGURE A

A product of today's technical world, this industrial-looking robot is programmed and ready to go. You don't need to be an electronics genius to make a copy.

DESCRIPTION: Sensor headgear and metallic slip-on body.

MATERIALS: 3 pieces of red, blue, or yellow poster board; 4 yds. silver Con-Tact paper; 1 yd. black and ¼ yd. each red, blue, and yellow Con-Tact paper; 2 flexible straws; staples; hole punch; black shoelaces (optional).

PREPARATIONS: Enlarge the body and headgear pattern pieces in figures B and C onto newspaper or brown wrapping paper; cut out. Cover 1 side of 2 pieces of poster board with silver Con-Tact paper. Trace body pattern onto paper side of each covered poster board; cut out. Trace headgear pieces onto remaining poster board; cut out. Trace 6 backwards 1's and six 0's, using the pattern in figure F, onto yellow Con-Tact paper. Cut an 11-×-10-in., a 2-×-22-in., and a ⅝-×-18-in. rectangle and two 4¼-in.-diameter circular discs from black Con-Tact paper. Cut ½-×-12-in. and ⅜-×-12-in. strips of yellow, blue, and red Con-Tact paper and two 24-×-27-in. and one 2½-×-18-in. rectangles from silver Con-Tact paper.

TO MAKE HEADGEAR: Using scissors, make a small slit on the short, top end of each straw. Slip the cut straw end onto the barbell-shaped headpiece, positioning as shown in figure D; tape ends flat on front and back. Peel backing from one 7-×-24-in. rectangle of silver Con-Tact paper and lay flat, adhesive side up. Center and secure barbell-shaped headpiece onto Con-Tact paper; trim along poster board edges, being careful not to cut the straws. Repeat this procedure to cover the other side of the headpiece. To create audio sensor, punch 2 circles on each black Con-Tact paper disc as shown in figure D.

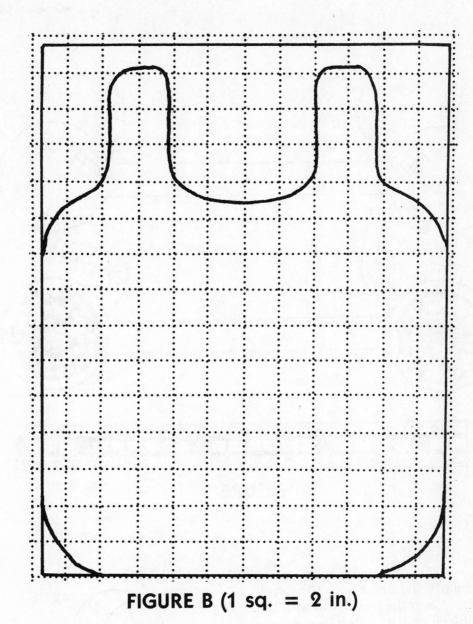

FIGURE B (1 sq. = 2 in.)

FIGURE C (1 sq. = 1½ in.)

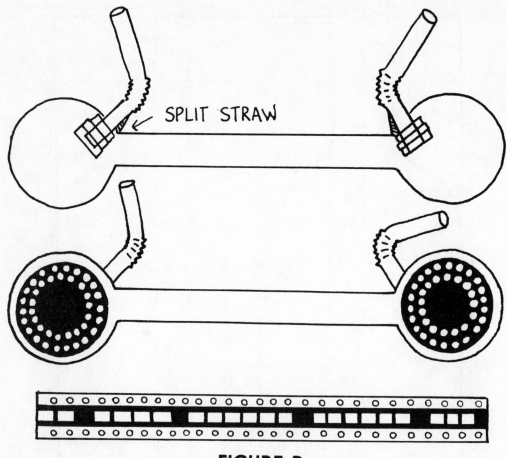

SPLIT STRAW

FIGURE D

Center and secure the discs onto the head-piece as shown. Cover the headband with the 2½-×-18-in. piece of silver Con-Tact paper; trim along poster board edges. Then, center and adhere the ⅝-×-18-in. black Con-Tact paper rectangle on top of the covered head-band. Using colored ⅜-×-12-in. strips, cut and adhere ½ in. pieces in a random pattern on top of the black strip as shown in figure D. Punch holes along the band edges, ½ in. apart (figure D). Staple the disc piece to the headband as shown in figure E. Punch holes at the ends of the band and tie closed to fit around the head with a piece of round-cord elastic.

FIGURE E

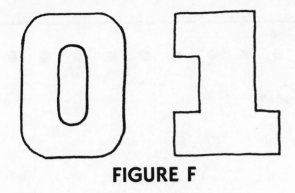

FIGURE F

TO MAKE BODY: Position and adhere the 10-×-11-in. black Con-Tact paper rectangle onto the metallic body front as shown in figure G. Center and adhere the numbers (figure F), in groupings of 4, on the black rectangle. Position and adhere the 2-×-22-in. black Con-Tact paper rectangle 2 in. up from the bottom edge; trim at sides. Using the colored Con-Tact paper strips, cut and create patterns of rectangles and squares as for the headband and secure on lower black strip (figure G). Punch holes around the front and back edges, ½ in. in from edge and approximately 1 in. apart. Staple front and back together to fit as shown (figure G). If desired, secure sides together by lacing through the front and back holes with shoelacing; tie.

ADULT SIZING: No alterations are necessary, although you can lengthen the body if desired. To do this, you will need to tape 2 pieces of poster board together for the front and back. The tape will be concealed by silver Con-Tact paper.

SUGGESTIONS: Dark or shiny, irridescent clothes lend the perfect foil to this high-tech costume. For added fun, fluorescent tape strips can be added in bands to your clothes.

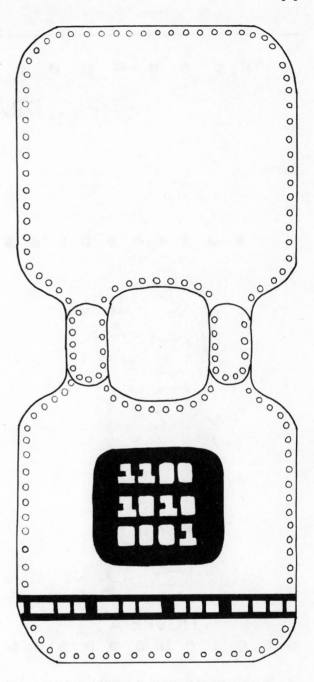

FIGURE G

DRAGON

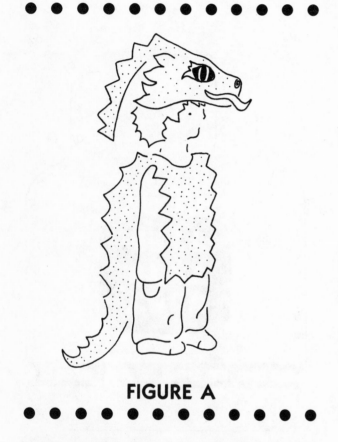

FIGURE A

This fire-tongued dragon is a truly good-looking "fellow," even from the back. Catch him on the run, and you'll see a spiny trail!

DESCRIPTION: Dragon headdress and spiny-backed felt slip-on body.

MATERIALS: 1 piece of green poster board; 1 yd. 72-in.-wide matching green felt; 2 squares of dark pink and 1 square each of blue and purple felt; small piece of white Con-

Tact paper, jumbo rickrack, or felt (for teeth); glue; round-cord elastic; double-stick tape.

PREPARATIONS: Enlarge body front, back, head, mouth, and teeth patterns as shown in figures B and C onto newspaper or brown wrapping paper; cut out. Trace the 4 eye pieces (figure D); cut out. Following the layout plan in figures B and C, first cut a 30-×-43-in. rectangle from the corner of the green felt, fold it, and pin the back pattern on it as shown; cut out. Next, lay the body pattern on the remaining piece of felt; cut out. Trace the head pattern twice and one ½-×-2-in. and two 1-in.-square stiffeners from green poster board; cut out, being careful when making the interior head cut near the spines. Using the mouth (figure C) and eye (figure D) patterns, pin and cut 2 tongues from dark pink felt, teeth from white felt (or rickrack or paper), 2 eye bases from green felt, 2 eyes from blue felt, 2 eye ovals from dark pink felt, and 2 pupils from purple felt. Also cut two 1½-in. ovals from dark pink felt for the nostrils.

TO MAKE HEADDRESS: Lay one face out flat. Tape ½-×-2-in. stiffener at first spine base as shown in figure E. Then, apply double-stick tape along the front half of the face and spine area, starting above the ears, as shown (figure E). Align and adhere second face/spine piece to the taped face/spine. Using a small piece of double-stick tape, secure 1-in. stiffener piece inside lower back edge of both faces as shown in figure E. Make each eye, layering and gluing the eye base, eye, oval, and pupil. Position and glue the eye, tongue, and teeth on both faces. Spiral-cut the nos-

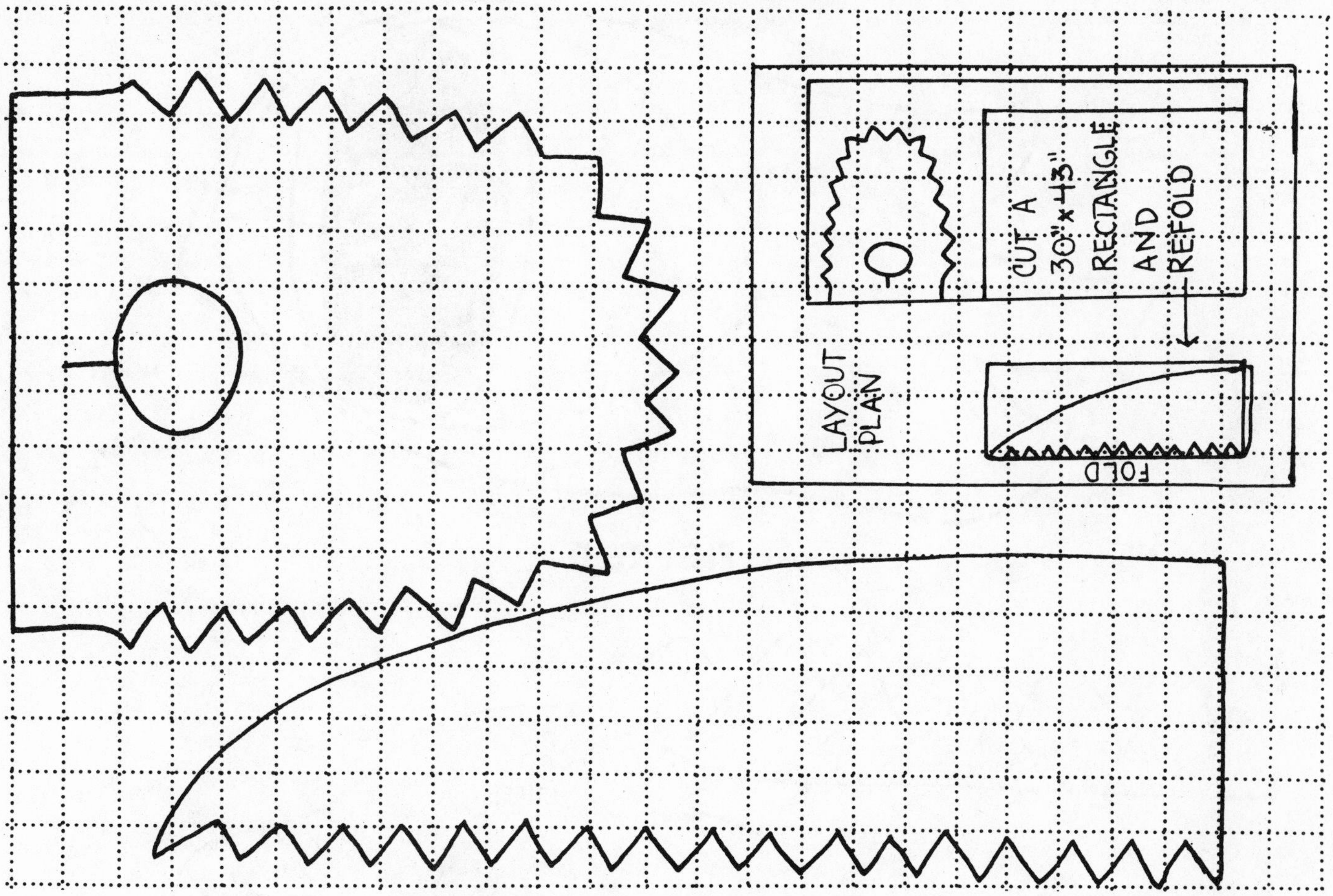
CUT A
30" x 43"
RECTANGLE
AND
REFOLD
LAYOUT
PLAN
FOLD

FIGURE B (1 sq. = 2 in.)

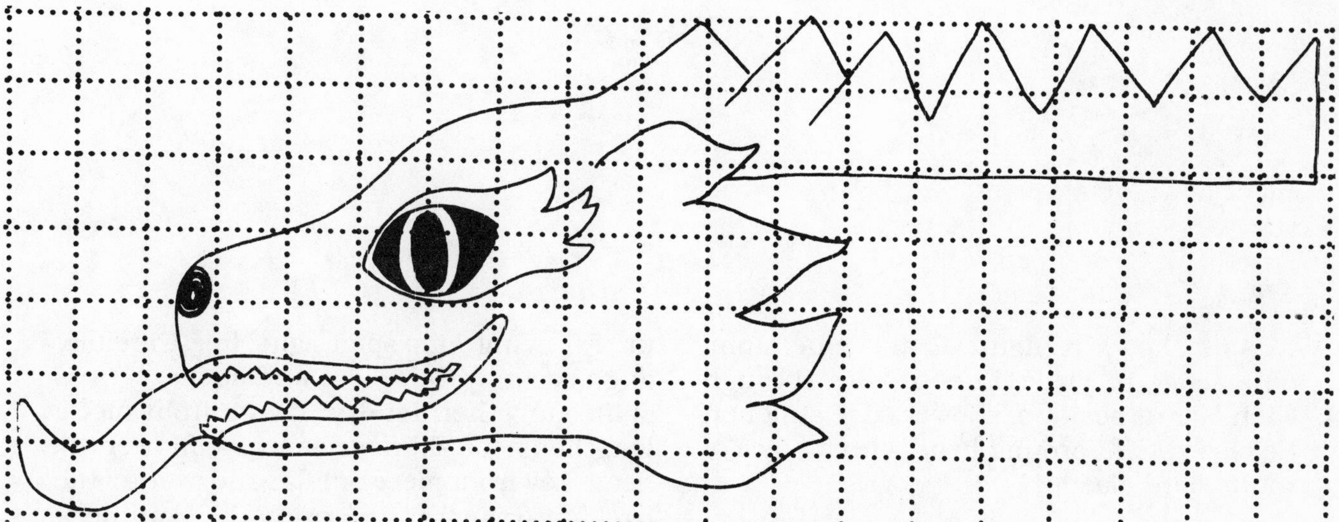

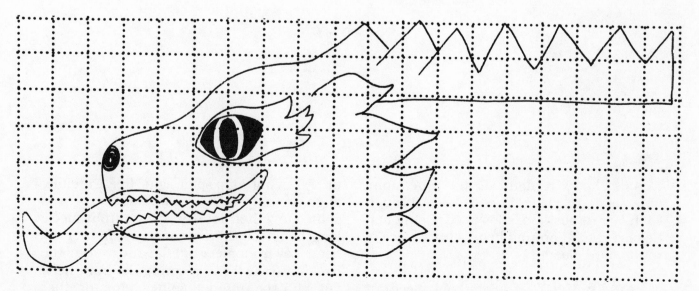

FIGURE C (1 sq. = 1½ in.)

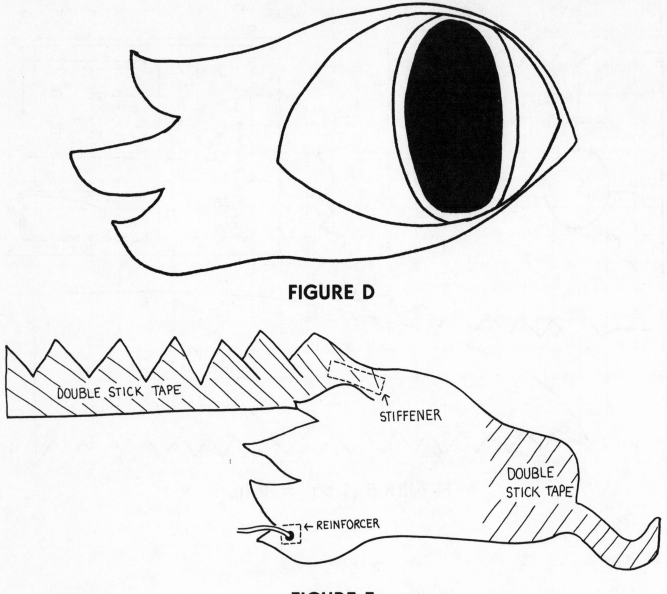

FIGURE D

DOUBLE STICK TAPE

STIFFENER

DOUBLE STICK TAPE

REINFORCER

FIGURE E

trils as shown in figure C and glue along outer edge in place. Punch holes through each face at position of lower edge stiffener; tie closed to fit around head with a piece of round-cord elastic.

TO MAKE BODY: Lay one back piece out flat. Squeeze glue onto piece as shown in fig-

ure F, leaving 3 top spines glue free. Carefully align second back piece and squeeze-press spines together; let dry. Try on front piece; lengthen neck slit if necessary to fit over the head. Lay front piece out flat and overlap the back onto the front, aligning the front neck cut with the unglued spines; glue together as shown in figure G and let dry.

ADULT SIZING: The slip-on body is the only piece that needs to be adjusted. Simply add to the length of the front and back pattern pieces to fit.

SUGGESTIONS: This traditional-looking dragon comes in green, but can be made in any color that is available in both poster board and felt. The dragon's spines can be jazzed up with glued-on sequins or other sparkly notions of your choice.

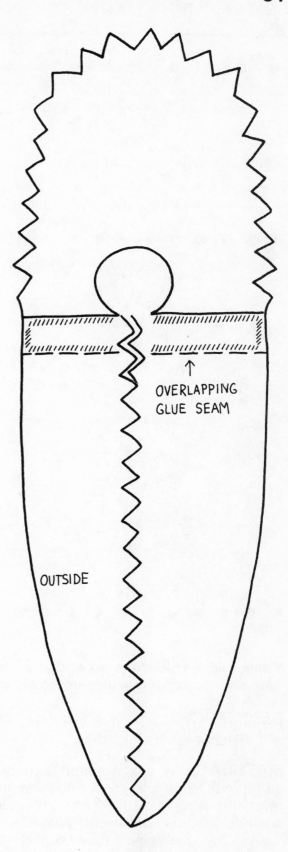

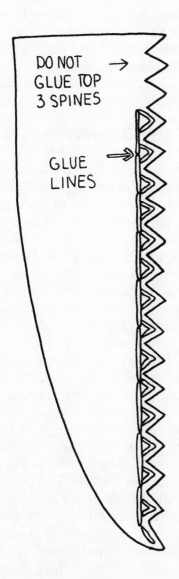

FIGURE F

FIGURE G

MERMAID

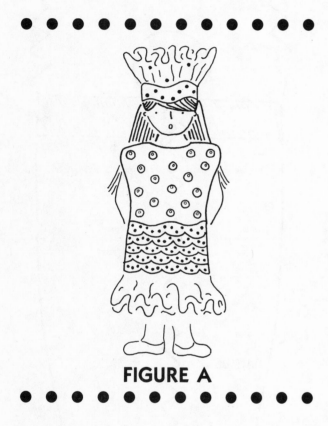

FIGURE A

A shimmering vision from out of the sea, this mermaid has no trouble getting around on land.

DESCRIPTION: Sea foam headband and shimmery felt slip-on body.

MATERIALS: ¾ yd. green and ¼ yd. blue 72-in.-wide felt; 6 yds. green fine-mesh netting; blue poster board; 50+ (1 bag) green and blue ½-in. sequins; twenty 20MM flat silver sequins; glue; staples; round-cord elastic; ribbon (optional).

PREPARATIONS: Enlarge body, wave, and headband patterns in figures B and C onto newspaper or brown wrapping paper; cut out. Following the layout in figure B, pin body pattern once and the wave pattern twice onto green felt; cut out. Pin and cut 3 waves from blue felt, using wave pattern (figure B). Trace headband pattern onto blue poster board; cut out. Cut net into 2 equal pieces (3 yds. each).

TO MAKE HEADBAND: Gather 1 piece of netting into accordion folds to reduce its size to 16 in. (most of the length of the band). Staple folded edge of netting to the headband, 1 in. in from the ends and at 2-in. intervals (figure D). Lay band out flat. On right side, glue green sequins on band in random fashion, covering staple ends when possible. Add 12 to 15 blue sequins to the outermost layers of netting, using double-stick tape (optional). Punch holes near the ends and tie around head to fit with a piece of round-cord elastic.

TO MAKE BODY: Lay body piece out flat, as shown in figure G. Cut a 4-in. slit at center back neck edge (when you wear the slip-on body, the slit will be in the back). Try the body on the wearer and lengthen the slit if necessary to fit over the head. Lay body piece out flat again. Working from the bottom up, position the upper edge of 1 blue wave 2 in. from the bottom edge of the body; trim wave at side edge. Using a thin line of glue along upper edge only, secure wave to body (figure E). Repeat procedure, positioning and gluing upper edge of green wave 2 in. from upper edge of blue wave; repeat procedure, alter-

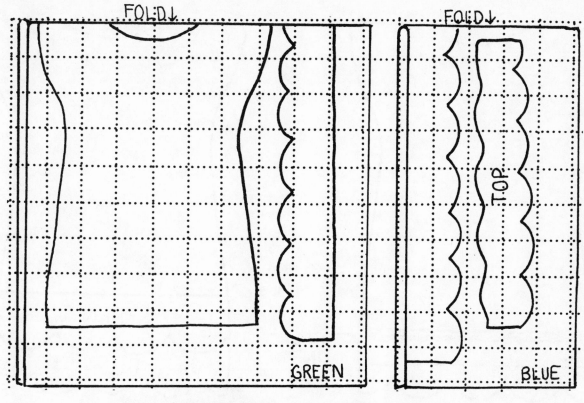

FIGURE B (1 sq. = 2½ in.)

FIGURE C (1 sq. = 2½ in.)

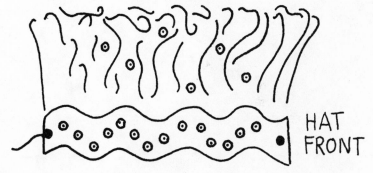

HAT FRONT

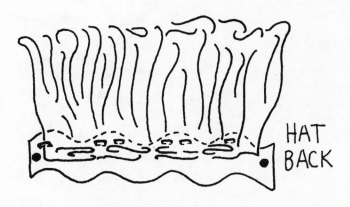

HAT BACK

FIGURE D

nating colors, until all 5 waves are attached. Cut remaining netting into 3 pieces of equal length. Fold each piece in half crosswise and hand-gather each piece along the crosswise fold. Lift and pin lower blue wave back onto the body; apply a thin line of glue along body edge close to upper edge of wave. Place folded edge of gathered netting onto glue line, positioning center section first and then the 2 side sections. Apply a thin line of glue near folded edge of wave, remove pin, and press wave down onto netting (figure F). Weight down until dry. Glue sequins onto body as shown, green on blue waves, blue on green, and silver on the upper body (figure G).

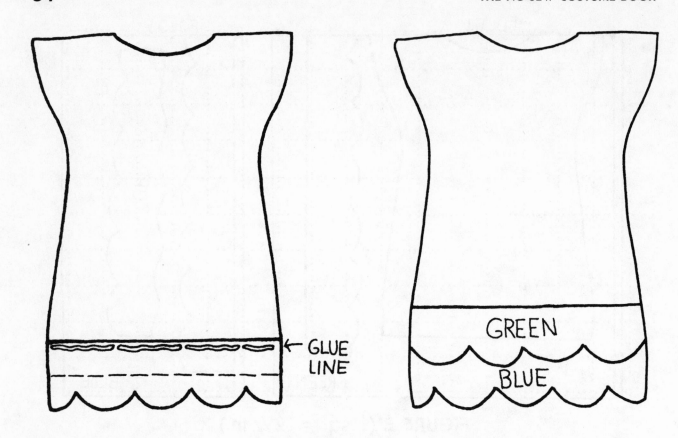

FIGURE E

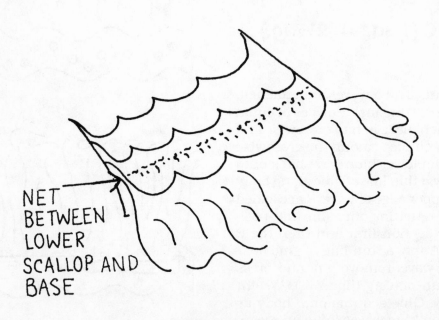

FIGURE F

ADULT SIZING: Alterations are not necessary, unless you want a full-length (below knee) body. For this, simply lengthen the body pattern and allow for extra felt if necessary.

SUGGESTIONS: For a more fitted look, you can attach the front and back together at the sides. To do this, punch a hole 1 in. in from the side edge to match on front and back of both sides; lace a ribbon through and tie closed.

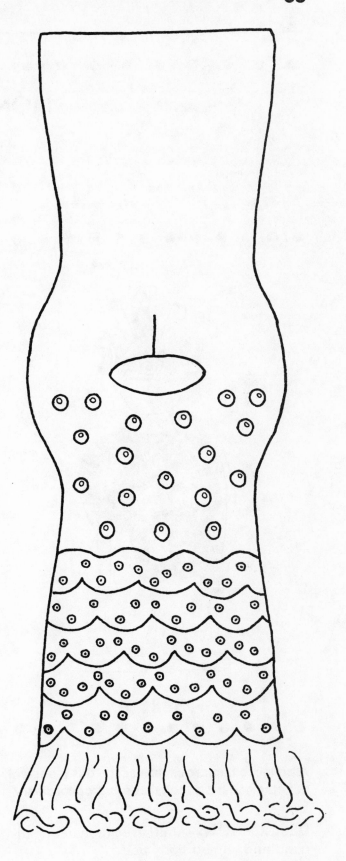

FIGURE G

MONSTER

FIGURE A

A bit more humorous than scary, this monster, nonetheless, has a look that's far from ordinary.

DESCRIPTION: Multi-eyed monster headband and slip-on body pelt.

MATERIALS: 1½ yds. brown or black fun fur; 1 small plastic Slinky; 8 or more green, screw-back cat's-eyes or large wiggle eyes; brown or black poster board; red or other contrasting-color poster board; small piece of silver Con-Tact paper (preferably) or aluminum foil; double-stick tape; glue; staples; round-cord elastic.

PREPARATIONS: Enlarge body, base headband and ear band, and ear patterns in figures B and C onto newspaper or brown wrapping paper; extend headband arrows an equal amount on each side to a finished length of 18 in. Cut out all pieces. Following the layout in figure B, pin the body pattern onto a single layer of fur; cut out. Trace the base headband pattern, 2 ears (including interior spiral cuts), and a 2-in. circle for the tongue onto red poster board and the ear band pattern onto brown or black poster board; cut out. Cover a large (6-in.) scrap of poster board with silver Con-Tact paper and cut it into 2-in. (approximately) irregularly shaped triangles. Cut the Slinky into 6 to 8 pieces.

TO MAKE HEADBAND: Beginning with the ear band, curl the center projection into a tube and staple it in place (figure D). Attach each spiral-cut ear piece to the ear position, using double-stick tape along the outermost edge to secure. Gently pull unattached ear spirals out from the ear band, forming a 3-D coil. Center and align ear band onto headband; secure, using double-stick tape, leaving the ear flaps free. Curl center and left-side

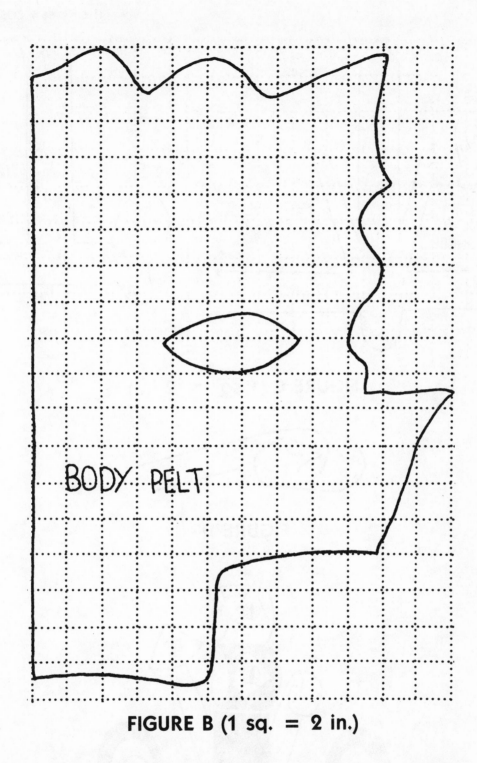

FIGURE B (1 sq. = 2 in.)

headband projections into a tube; staple in place as shown in figure D. Spiral-cut the 2-in. red poster board circle (same as for ear) and attach along outermost edge to mouth position, using double-stick tape. Coil, same as for ears (figure E). To create eyes, use scissors to carefully punch a small hole in the center of 4 metallic triangles. Push a cat's-eye screw-back through each hole. Then, punch a hole on the headband projections and push screw-back through as shown in figure E. Secure in place with metal clasp that's provided with eye (which threads on the screw-back) or by putting small pieces of double-stick tape under the triangles. Lace one cut Slinky "earring" onto each coiled ear.

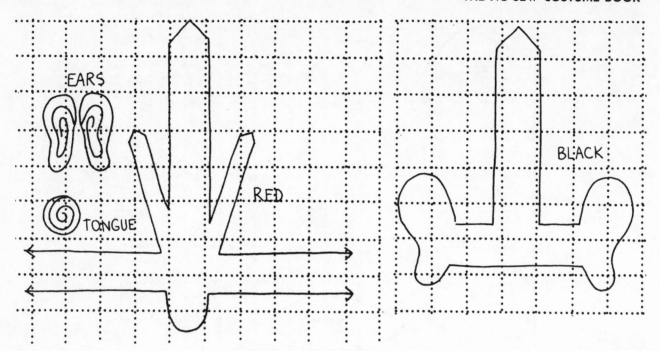

EARS

RED

TONGUE

BLACK

FIGURE C (1 sq. = 2 in.)

FIGURE D

FIGURE E

TO MAKE BODY: Create several eye pieces, same as for headband. Attach the eye pieces to the body front, positioning as shown (figure F), by poking small holes in the fur backing with scissors or by just pushing the screw-back through. Secure eye pieces on back with clasps provided. Position and secure Slinkys on fur, making a hole same as for eyes and sliding a coil of the Slinky through to the back. Work with the Slinky on front, stretching and twisting it to form the desired, wacky appearance.

ADULT SIZING: No alterations necessary.

SUGGESTIONS: Using the fur remnant, you can make a hand flap—furry covering for top of hand—by cutting an irregular shape to fit the upper hand. Punch 2 holes at the wrist edge, lace a piece of round-cord elastic through the holes, and tie closed to fit.

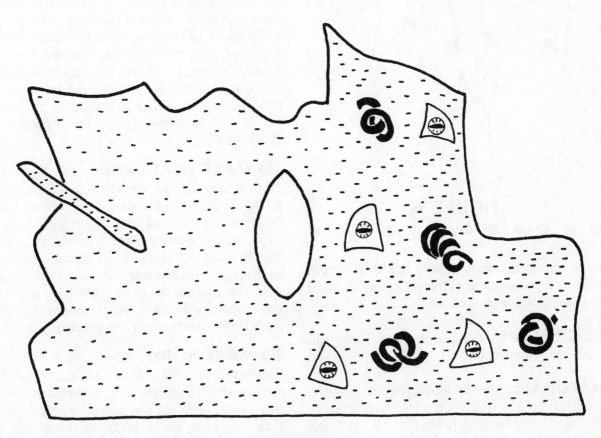

FIGURE F

FAERIE

FIGURE A

From out of a dream comes this diaphanous wisp of a costume, unbelievably easy to make and enchanting to look at.

DESCRIPTION: Beribboned headband and icicle net slip-on body.

MATERIALS: 6 yds. white (cut into 1½-yd. lengths) or 1½ yds. each of 4 coordinating colors of netting (preferably fine mesh); ½ yd. white or coordinating-color 72-in.-wide felt;

5 yds. of ¼- to ½-in.-wide ribbon; decorations for ribbon ends—flowers, stick-on stars, etc.; rubber band or tie.

PREPARATIONS: Enlarge body and collar patterns in figure B onto newspaper (attached together) or brown wrapping paper; cut out. Align and place 4 single layers of netting together; randomly pin through all layers— this will help prevent slippage. Fold the pinned netting in half, and following the layout in figure B, pin the body pattern to the netting, pinning along all pattern edges; cut out along outer, solid lines only. Remove pattern, but keep body netting layers randomly pinned together. Save netting remnants for the headband. Pin petal collar to folded felt (figure B); cut out along outer edges and inner circle. On one collar, using a hole punch, punch holes ½ in. from petal points as indicated by X's in figure B. Cut ribbon into 7 pieces.

TO MAKE HEADBAND: Tie 1 piece of ribbon around the wearer's head as shown in figure A, tying it loosely enough so it can be slipped off the head but still feels comfortable on the wearer; make a knot and remove the headband. Gather up some of the remaining netting in a small bunch and secure it to the headband at the knot by knotting the ribbon around it. Tie a bow and glue or stick on decorations at ribbon ends (figure A).

TO MAKE BODY: The body is made by sandwiching and gluing netting between 2 collars and trimming away the netting at the neck hole area for the head opening. To do this, working on a large surface, lay the unpunched collar out flat. Center and posi-

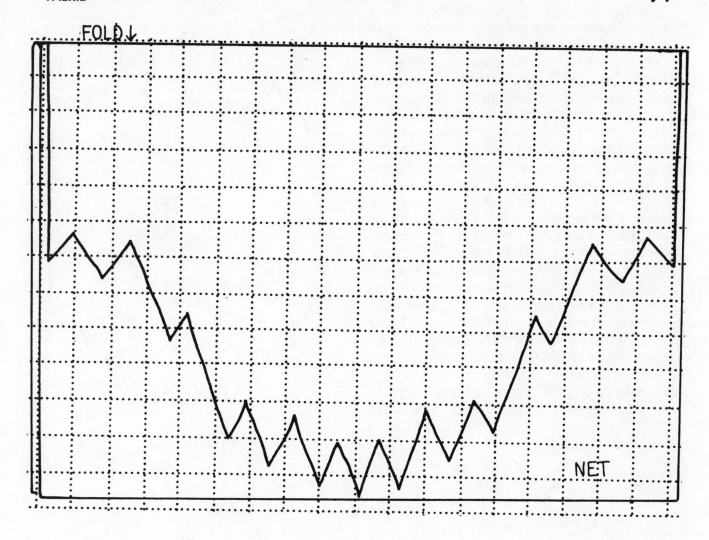

FOLD↓

NET

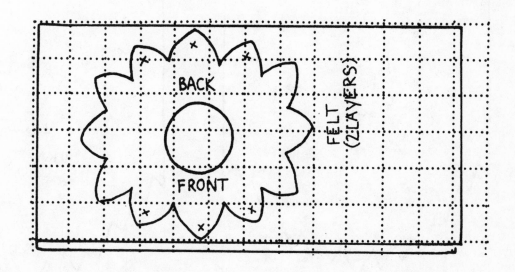

BACK

FRONT

FELT (2 LAYERS)

FIGURE B (1 sq. = 2½ in.)

tion the pinned, layered body piece on top of the collar, orienting the front and back of the collar to the body as shown in figure C. Remove the pins in the collar area, then generously apply glue through the netting onto the collar, leaving the petal points glue free (figure D). Align the outer edges of the remaining collar piece on the glued collar, sandwiching the netting in between. Squeeze-press together (figure E). Before glue dries, stick 1 end of each ribbon length through the petal-point hole, approximately 1 to 2 in., lifting the petal point to do this (figure F). Apply a bit more glue on petal underside to hold ribbon in place; finger-press petal point flat and let dry. Attach decorations to ribbon ends (same as for headband), gluing in place to the top layer of netting or to the ribbon end only for a dangling effect; let dry (figure G). Trim away netting from neck hole area. Then, cut a slit in neckline at center back as shown, cutting through all layers, but not extending the slit beyond the collar edge (figure G). Try

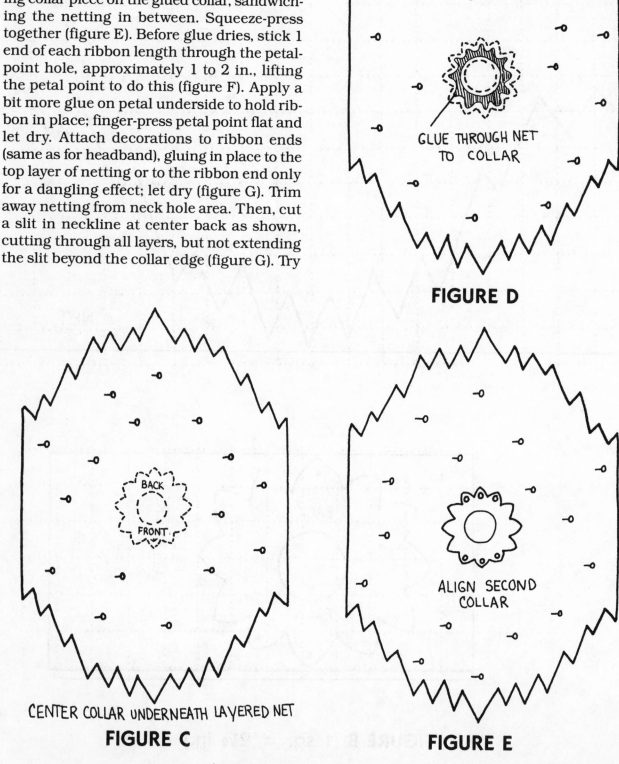

GLUE THROUGH NET
TO COLLAR

FIGURE D

BACK

FRONT

CENTER COLLAR UNDERNEATH LAYERED NET

FIGURE C

ALIGN SECOND
COLLAR

FIGURE E

body on wearer and extend slit if necessary to fit over the head. While still on, carefully cut angled slashes—approximately 9 in. long—along the bottom edge through all layers, lifting the ribbons out of the way and holding the netting taut (figure G). These slashes allow for easier movement and the optional use of a belt. Remove all pins.

ADULT SIZING: The slip-on body can be worn very effectively as is over a flowing gown or dress, or it can be lengthened. To do this, make the body pattern, hold it up to the wearer, and determine how long you want the body to be. Measure the difference in length and double it (to account for front and back). Cut the pattern in half along the straight edge and add a piece of paper between the 2 cut edges equal to the width and the determined extra length; tape in place. Allow for extra length when purchasing netting and continue same as above.

SUGGESTIONS: Additional decorations (stars, hearts, flowers) can be added to the netting layers as desired. Ribbons and netting can be tied together for wristlets.

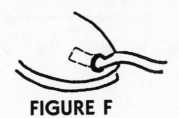

FIGURE F

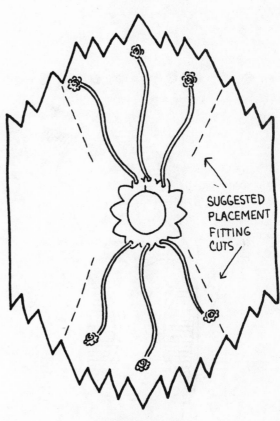

SUGGESTED PLACEMENT FITTING CUTS

FIGURE G

UNICORN

FIGURE A

In a world of their own, unicorns will ride on, forever capturing the imaginations of young and old alike. Simple, but beautiful, this unicorn can be ultrafeminine or dramatically masculine, depending on the colors used.

DESCRIPTION: Unicorn head and felt slip-on body.

MATERIALS: ½ yd. white and ¼ yd. pink 72-in.-wide felt; 2 sheets pink poster board (close in color to felt); 3½ yds. turquoise or purple silk cording; 5 yds. gold strung sequins; gold glitter (optional); 2 large wiggle eyes; glue; double-stick tape; hole punch.

PREPARATIONS: Enlarge body, saddle, and wing pattern pieces shown in figures B and C and the head and mane patterns in figure D onto newspaper or brown wrapping paper; cut out. Following the layout in figure B, pin body and mane pattern to folded white felt and saddle pattern to folded pink felt; cut out. Carefully cut neck hole in the body and save the circular remnant for use on wing piece. Trace and cut wings, 2 headpieces, and a 2-×-18-in. rectangular band from pink poster board.

TO MAKE HEAD: Glue eyes and mane in place to create a right and left face as shown in figure D. Draw a fine line of glue along outline of each mane and lay silk cording or strung sequins (string side down) on glue line; trim ends and let dry. To create gold horn, cover horn with a thin layer of glue and apply glitter and/or loose sequins (unstrung) generously to horn; let dry, shake to remove excess. To construct hat, lay 1 face, wrong side up, and apply pieces of double-stick tape to cover the facial area in front of the neck and all of the horn. Place the 2 faces together, right sides out and edges aligned; finger-press to secure together. Fold poster board band in half and place between attached face pieces, along lower edge and starting approximately 6¼ in. in from the back edge, as

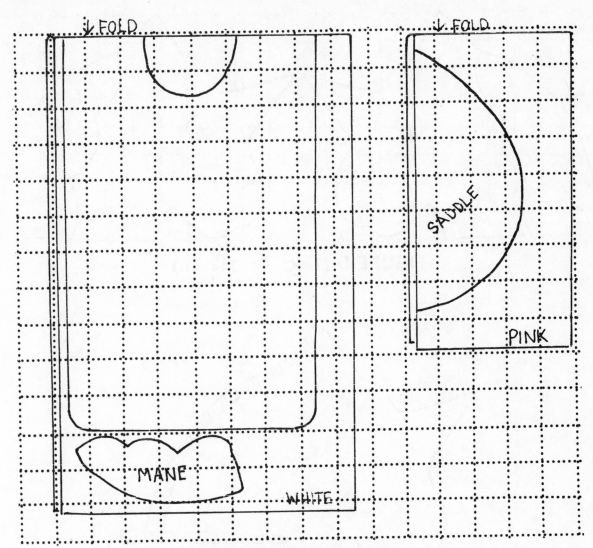

FIGURE B (1 sq. = 2 in.)

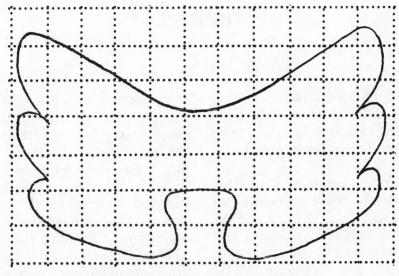

FIGURE C (1 sq. = 2 in.)

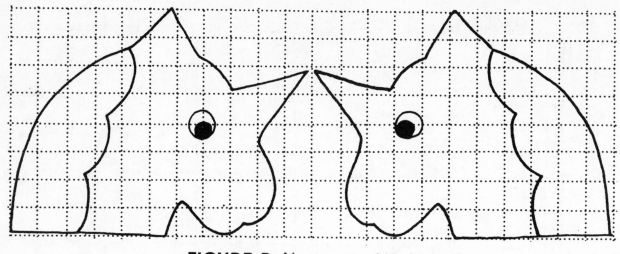

FIGURE D (1 sq. = 1¼ in.)

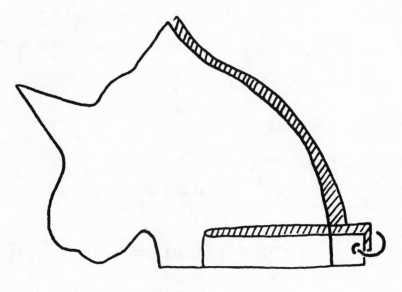

FIGURE E

shown in figure E. Using double-stick tape, secure band in place. Punch holes at the ends of the band and tie closed to fit around the head with a piece of round-cord elastic.

TO MAKE BODY: Lay body out flat. Cut a 3-in. slit as shown in figure F at center of circle edge (when you wear the body, the slit will be in the back). Try body on wearer and extend slit if necessary to fit over the head. To make saddle, lay and glue pink saddle pieces in place as shown. For each saddle piece, draw a thin line of glue 1 in. in from the rounded edge on saddle, following the curve (figure F). Affix strung sequins, string side down, onto glue line; trim. Draw a thin line of glue onto white body along rounded saddle edge; affix silk cording onto glue line, trim, and let dry. To make wings, work on one side at a time, and starting at the center, draw a glue line 1 in. from the outer wing edge; affix strung sequins onto glue and trim (figure F). Trim felt neck hole remnant to a 4- × - 6-in. oval. Lay wings onto body back, sequin side up, and secure to body, gluing as shown. Cover felt oval with glue and lay over center of wings, hiding sequin ends and overlapping onto body piece (figure F). Cover with plastic wrap and weight down with books until dry.

ADULT SIZING: No alterations are necessary, although you may lengthen the body if you wish.

SUGGESTIONS: For a more dramatic, masculine look, make a black felt body and head with red or purple details.

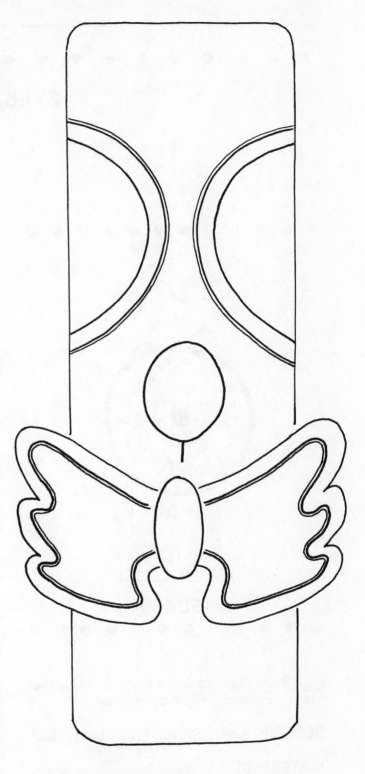

FIGURE F

EYEBALL

FIGURE A

Always on the watch, this bulging, bloodshot eyeball catches people by surprise.

DESCRIPTION: Slip-on bloodshot eyeball.

MATERIALS: 3 pieces white poster board; 1 yd. red and ¼ yd. black Con-Tact paper; 1 sheet metallic blue wrapping paper or ¼ yd. blue Con-Tact paper; double-stick tape; red marking pen; ¼-in. or round-cord elastic; staples; hole punch.

PREPARATIONS: Measure and draw 2 rounded ovals on white poster board, one 22 × 24 in., the other 18 × 20 in., and 2 strips, each 9 × 26 in. On the 18-×-20-in. oval only, extend the side edges out 3 × 3 in., forming 2 tabs as shown in figure B; cut out all pieces. Measure and cut a 3-in. and an 8-in. circle from black Con-Tact paper and a 7¾-in. circle from metallic blue paper. Cut 8 slightly curved slivers of Con-Tact paper, approximately 2 in. long, for detailing the iris of the eye. Trace outer edge of the 22-×-24-in. oval onto red Con-Tact paper, piecing as necessary. Measure in 2 in. from the outline and cut out, forming an eye ring.

TO MAKE EYEBALL: Position and affix large Con-Tact paper circle in the middle of the large oval eyeball. Center the blue paper iris on top of the black circle and secure with small pieces of double-stick tape. Center and affix small black circle (pupil) onto the blue iris. Position and affix Con-Tact paper slivers on the iris, radiating from the pupil (figure C). Using red marker, draw broken blood vessels (jagged lines that resemble tree branches) on the white eye area as shown. Turn the eye over to the wrong side. Fold each poster board 9-×-26-in. strip into thirds, forming a 3-×-26-in. strip; fold up 1½ to 2 in. on each end of 1 strip. Center strip with folded ends on back of eye, so it goes across the eye (shorter, 22-in. width) and the fold lines are aligned with the side edges; staple the ends to the eye 1 in. in from the edge (figure D). The eye will bulge outward. Lay the remaining strip lengthwise over the first, on center and with ends aligned with upper and lower edge of eye; staple ends to eye (figure D). Draw broken blood vessels on remaining oval with tabs (the back of the eyeball). Position oval on top of the crossed strips, slipping tabs between the eye and the folded strip ends on the sides; staple all 3 layers together close to the edge (figure E).

Punch 2 holes along the upper edge of back eyeball, 1 in. from the edge and 5 in. from center on either side. Tie a 20-in. piece of elastic (or doubled round-cord elastic) through 1 hole, weave it under the strip at the top of the front eye, and then pull it through the other hole and tie loosely. Slide the eyeball onto the wearer, over the head; the crossed strips will rest on the front upper body. Adjust elastic to fit and tie securely (figure F).

ADULT SIZING: No changes are necessary.

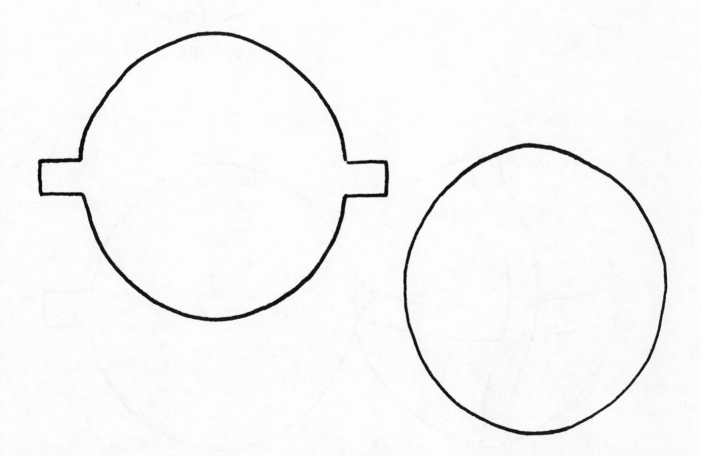

FIGURE B

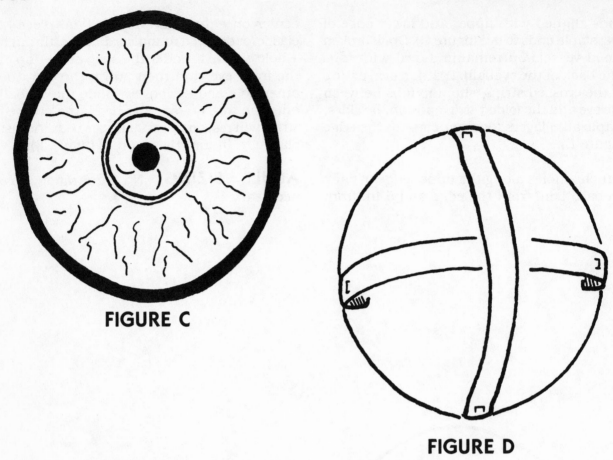

FIGURE C

FIGURE D

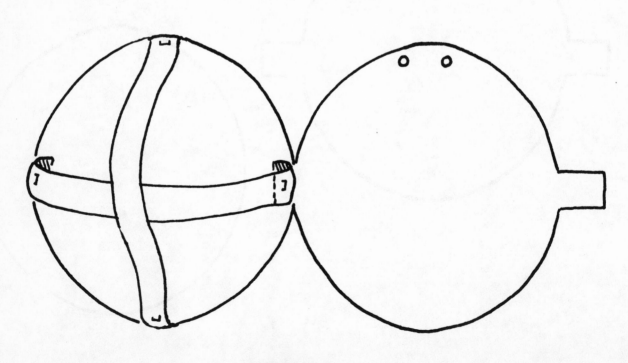

FIGURE E

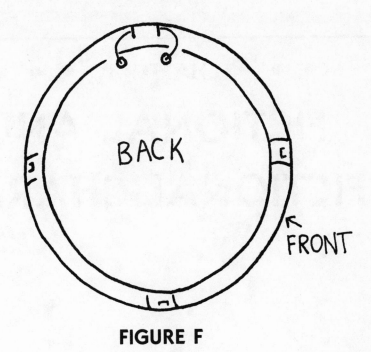

FIGURE F

• • • • CHAPTER IV • • • •

FICTIONAL AND NONFICTIONAL CHARACTERS

CLEOPATRA

FIGURE A

A figure from the past, the beauty and allure of Cleopatra are captured with simplicity in this colorful and comfortable costume (see illustration on front cover).

DESCRIPTION: "Hair" band/felt wig and felt, "jewelled" slip-on tunic.

MATERIALS: ½ yd. navy, ¼ yd. gold (or 3 squares), ½ yd. white, and ¼ yd. black 72-in.-wide felt (if navy felt is not available by the yard and gold is, reverse these yardages); 1 or 2 squares turquoise felt; metallic notions, such as 1½ yds. strung gold sequins, metallic gold slick fabric pen, or glitter; jewel notions, such as glue-on rubies, rhinestones, large sequins, or glitter; small piece of gold Con-Tact paper (optional); aluminum foil; 2-×-20-in. band of poster board or similar weight cardboard; round-cord elastic; staples; hole punch.

PREPARATIONS: Enlarge tunic and collar patterns (include dotted lines and numbers) shown in figures B and C onto newspaper or brown wrapping paper; cut out. Following the layout in figure B, pin tunic pattern onto folded white felt; cut out. Then pin collar, folded in half, onto folded navy felt as shown in figure B and cut out along outside lines

102

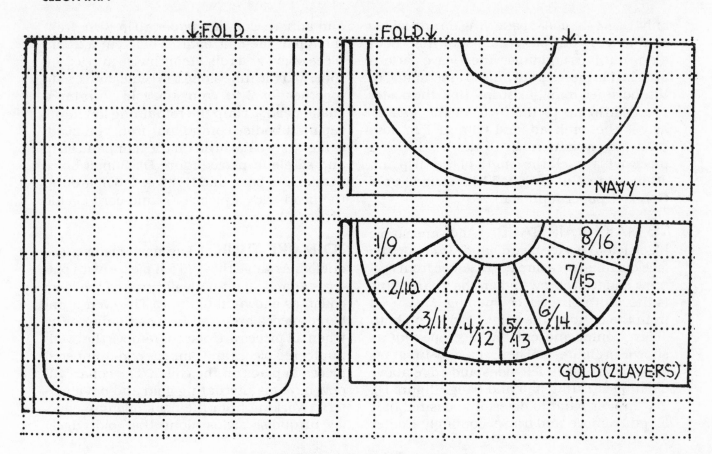

FIGURE B (1 sq. = 2 in.)

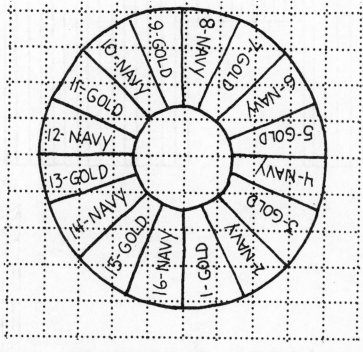

FIGURE C (1 sq. = 2 in.)

only. Using the collar pattern again and folded gold felt, lay out pattern as shown and cut along outlines and inner lines; leave pattern attached to pieces until time of assembly. Cut turquoise felt into ¼-in. strips. Hold the poster board strip up to the head of the wearer, across the forehead, and trim to 1 in. less than the circumference of the head. Cut a piece of black felt the length of the strip and 10 in. wide. Cut a 1¼-×-14-in. strip of gold Con-Tact paper (optional).

TO MAKE HAIR BAND:
Align and staple black felt to poster board band. To create the face opening, measure the distance from eyebrow end to eyebrow end on the wearer; this is the width of the face opening. Measured from the bottom, the height is 5 in. on both sides. Center and cut the face opening as shown in figure D. Then, make ½-in. grass cuts on the black felt sides and edge above opening, creating hair and bangs (figure D). Try on hair band to determine desired hair length, remove, and trim accordingly. Center

and adhere Con-Tact paper strip ¼ in. from the top of the hair band. Then, cut a 26-in. piece of foil and roll it lengthwise into a 2-in. tube; fold the tube along the center and crimp together for 2 in. from the fold, forming a snake head. Crimp the remaining foil into 2 separate bodies coming out from the head; center the snake head on the hair band strip and staple in place (figure D). Punch holes near end of band and tie closed to fit around the head with a piece of round-cord elastic (figure D).

TO MAKE TUNIC:
Lay navy collar piece out flat. Arrange the gold felt pieces (with patterns attached) numerically around the navy collar, as shown in figure C. The even-numbered pieces are used for positioning only; when all pieces are placed, remove the even-numbered pieces and glue the odd-numbered pieces in place on the collar. The collar will now have an alternating gold and navy pattern. Working from the neck opening edge, lay turquoise strips along the gold edges;

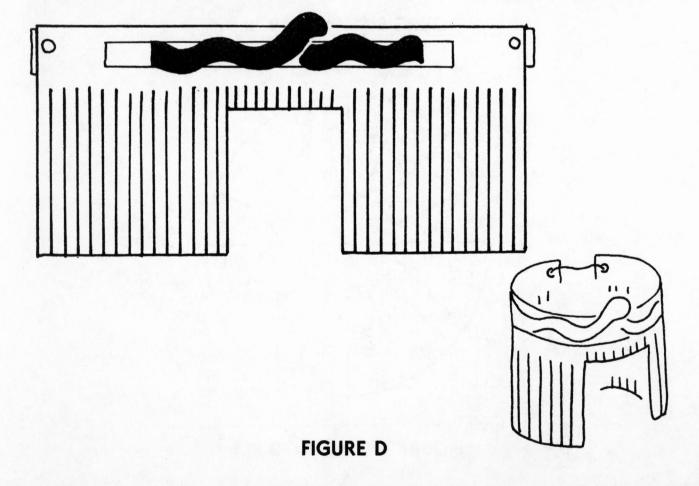

FIGURE D

trim along outer collar edges and glue in place (figure E). On each gold felt segment, draw a thin line of glue from the neck opening to the collar edge; lay strung sequins on glue, thread side down, trim, and gently finger-press to secure. Position and glue jewels, large sequins, or glitter (or, draw on jewels with slick fabric paint) in place on navy segments as shown in Figure E. To complete, lay the white felt tunic out flat. Position decorated collar on tunic, right side up and centered, and glue in place; let dry. Trim away tunic neck hole area along collar neck edge and cut a 4-in. slit along the center back neck edge—through both layers—as shown (figure F). Try tunic on wearer and extend slit if necessary to fit over the head.

ADULT SIZING: Use the full 72-in. felt width to make a longer version of the tunic.

SUGGESTIONS: Make foil snake arm bands and/or add a gold belt to the tunic.

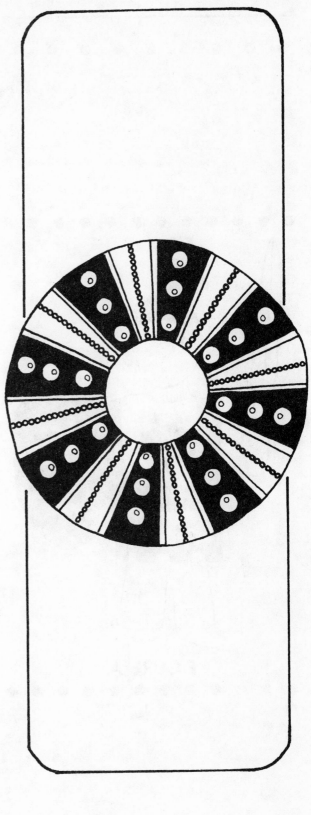

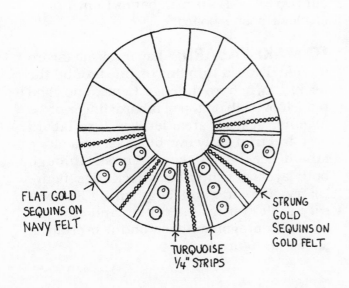

FLAT GOLD SEQUINS ON NAVY FELT

STRUNG GOLD SEQUINS ON GOLD FELT

TURQUOISE ¼" STRIPS

FIGURE E

FIGURE F

KNIGHT

Fearless and brave is the knight who wears the emblem of the double-headed dragon. Very little effort is required, however, to pull this garb together!

FIGURE A

DESCRIPTION: Double-headed dragon tabard and shield.

MATERIALS: ⅔ yd. black and ⅓ yd. red 72-in.-wide felt; 2 pieces black poster board; glue; tape; staples.

PREPARATIONS: Enlarge tabard, overbib, and dragon emblem as shown in figures B and C on newspaper or brown wrapping paper; cut out. Following the layouts in figure B, pin the tabard onto folded black felt and the overbib onto folded red felt; cut out. Pin and cut 1 dragon from remaining black felt and 1 or 2 dragons from red felt. Measure and cut two 2¼-×-14-in. arm bands from 1 piece of black poster board.

TO MAKE TABARD: Lay black felt tabard out flat. Draw a thin line of glue around the neck, ¼ in. in from the edge. Center and align red felt overbib on top of tabard; finger-press together at neck area; let dry. Turn tabard over and trim away overbib neck area along tabard neckline. Make a 4-in. slit through both layers at center back neck edge (figure E); try on wearer and lengthen slit if necessary to fit over head. Position and glue the black felt dragon emblem on the overbib as shown in figure E.

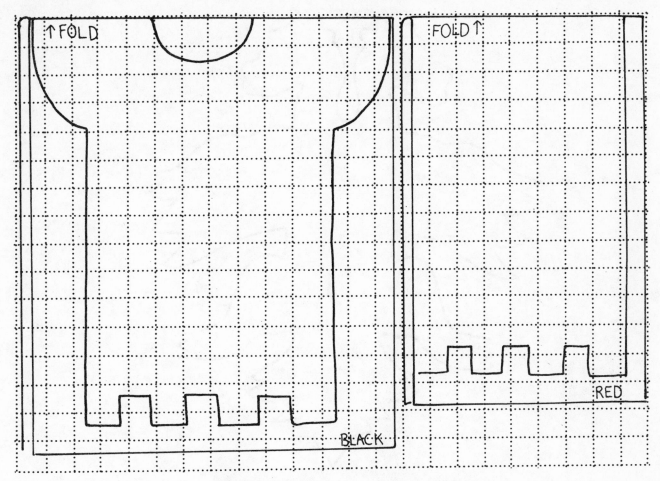

FIGURE B (1 sq. = 1½ in.)

TO MAKE SHIELD: Fold the uncut black poster board in half. Cut a shield shape, using the full width and height of the folded board, as shown in figure D. Position and staple ends of arm bands to the shield, stapling through 1 layer only; tape ends of bands to shield (figure D). Glue or staple the 2 shield layers together along the cut edges; let dry if glued. Position and glue 1 or 2 red dragon emblems on the shield front (figure D).

ADULT SIZING: No alterations are necessary, although you may lengthen the tabard if desired.

SUGGESTIONS: The remaining poster board can be used to make a sword or lance. For a shiny blade, cover with silver Con-Tact paper or foil. Other royal colors that are good choices for this costume are royal blue and black, purple and black, green and black, or purple and red.

FIGURE C

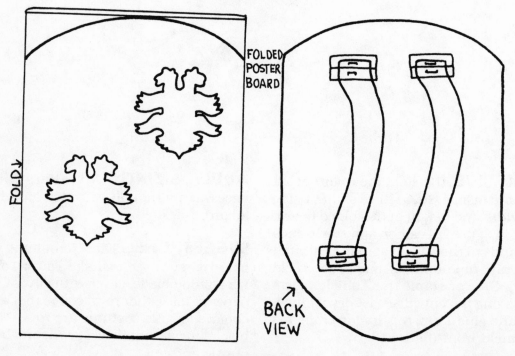

FIGURE D

FIGURE E

BALLERINA

FIGURE A

A new turn on a classic, this all-season ballerina costume comes with legs included, toe shoes and all. Its slip-on design allows for easy movement.

DESCRIPTION: Bow band and felt slip-on ballerina body.

MATERIALS: ⅔ yd. bright pink and ¼ yd. each of light pink, black, and white 72-in.-

wide felt; black or navy yarn; glue; strung sequins (optional); round-cord elastic.

PREPARATIONS: Enlarge body, collar, leg, and shoe patterns in figure B onto newspaper or brown wrapping paper; cut out. Following the layout in figure B, pin the body piece on a single layer of bright pink felt as shown; cut out. Fold the remaining bright pink felt, and following the layout, pin the collar onto it as shown; cut out. Pin legs to the folded white felt; cut out. Pin the shoe pattern to folded black felt; cut out shoes and three ⅝-×-16-in. strips for the shoe ties. For the headband, measure and cut a 1½-×-16-in. black felt rectangle and a 1-×-14-in. bright pink felt rectangle. For bows, cut twelve 1-×-4½-in. rectangles and one 1-×-6-in. rectangle plus a 2-×-14-in. belt from light pink felt. Cut one 1½-×-9-in. black felt rectangle for the belt bow.

TO MAKE HEADBAND: Center and glue the 1-×-14-in. pink rectangle on top of the 1½-×-16-in. black rectangle. Add a single strand of strung sequins—if desired—on center, using a thin line of glue to secure; let dry (figure C). On wrong side, reinforce each band end with a small square of poster board or cardboard; glue in place and let dry. Make a bow, using the 1-×-6-in. light pink felt rectangle; overlap the ends, glue, and press together to make a tube (figure D). Tie a 6-in. piece of black yarn around the middle of the tube tightly, knotting to make a bow (figure D). Glue the bow on front of band in position shown (figure C); let dry. Punch holes at band ends through the poster board; tie closed to fit around the head with a piece of round-cord elastic.

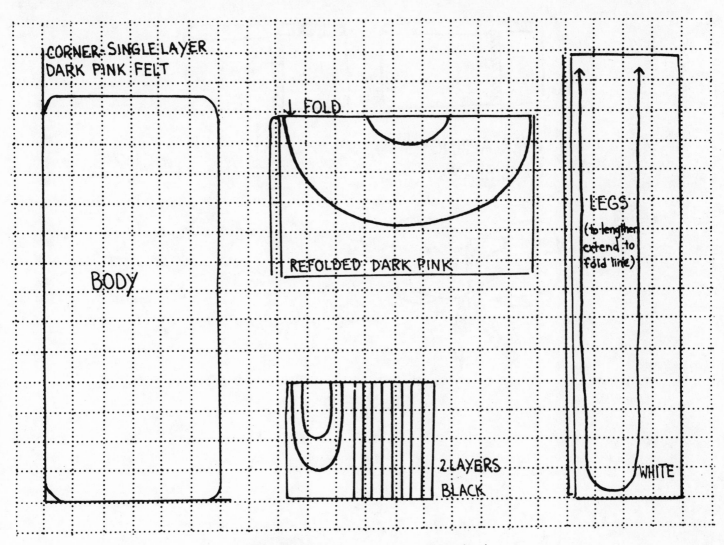

CORNER-SINGLE LAYER
DARK PINK FELT

BODY

↓ FOLD

REFOLDED DARK PINK

2 LAYERS
BLACK

LEGS
(to lengthen
extend to
fold line)

WHITE

FIGURE B (1 sq. = 2½ in.)

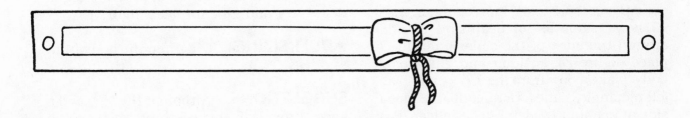

FIGURE C

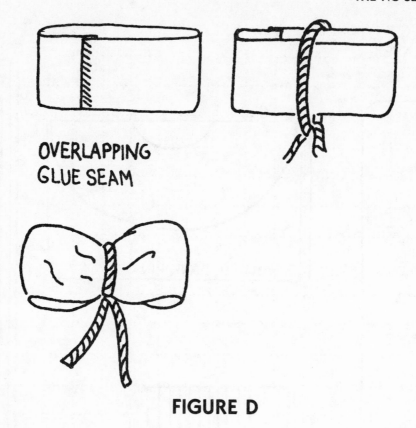

OVERLAPPING
GLUE SEAM

FIGURE D

TO MAKE BODY: Lay body piece out flat. Position open collar on body, centering and aligning the back edges; glue in place around neck hole, shoulder edges, and back edge of body; let dry. Cut away neck hole from body piece and cut a 4-in. slit at center back neck edge as shown in figure E. Try on, lengthening the slit if necessary to fit over head, and check the body length. If the length is longer than midthigh, shorten it, cutting off the excess. Using the 1-×-4½-in. rectangles, make 12 bows, same as for headband. Position around the edge of the collar and glue in place (figure E). Position and glue belt to body. Make a bow from the 1½-×-9-in. black felt rectangle, same as for headband; glue to side of belt and let dry. Decorate legs. Position and glue on shoes first, then laces (⅝-×-16-in. strips), crisscrossing them up the lower leg as shown (figure E). Cut remaining black strip into 4 equal pieces for leg ties. Position and glue these to wrong side of legs as shown in figure E. To determine the leg length, try the body on the wearer and hold the legs up so that the ballet slippers extend from the bottom of the body to the top of the wearer's feet. Pin legs in place with excess on wrong side of body. Remove costume and lay out flat, wrong side up. Trim leg if necessary and glue in place (figure E).

ADULT SIZING: Lengthen the body front and legs.

SUGGESTIONS: Although the legs add a special touch to this costume, they can be eliminated. The colors chosen are very feminine but can be changed to your liking.

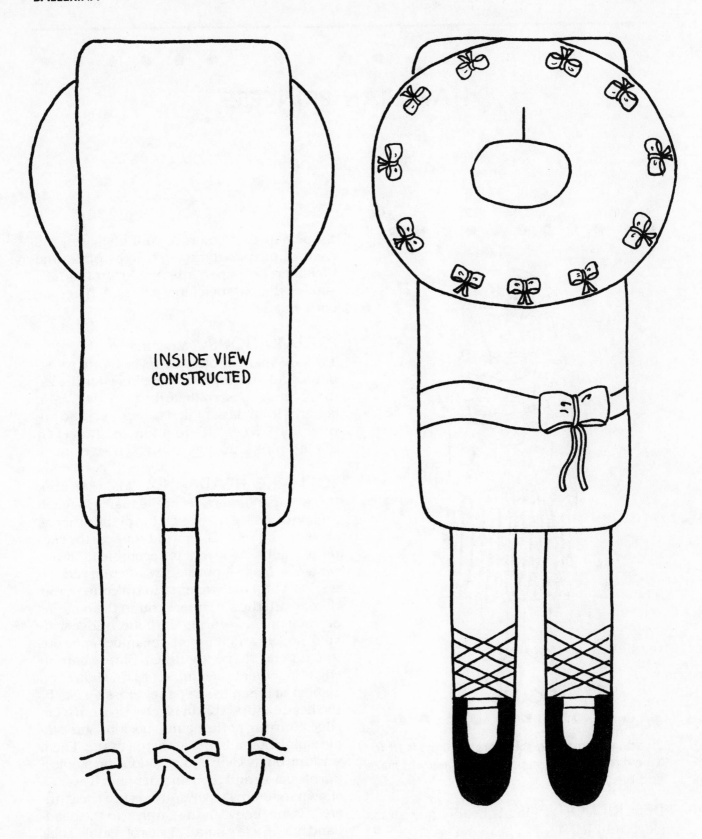

INSIDE VIEW
CONSTRUCTED

FIGURE E

HAWAIIAN PRINCESS

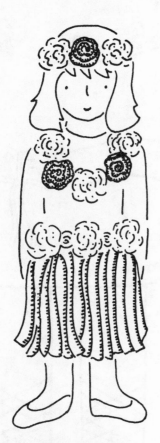

FIGURE A

Bursting with color, this floral delight is fit for a most royal Hawaiian princess. It's easy to make and easy to wear.

DESCRIPTION: Floral headband, grass skirt, and lei.

MATERIALS: 1 piece pink poster board; 3 sheets each of light green and dark pink

tissue paper (or colors of your choice); 1 roll each of purple, dark pink, light pink, and green crepe paper streamers; craft knife; staples; double-stick tape; hole punch; round-cord elastic.

PREPARATIONS: Measure and cut a 1½-×-16-in. headband, a 1¾-×-24-in. waistband, and a 10-in.-diameter circle (for the lei) from pink poster board; forty-five 5-in. squares from dark pink tissue paper; and approximately four 40- to 42-in. lengths each of both pinks, purple, and green streamers.

TO MAKE HEADBAND: Make 9 pink tissue paper flowers, using 4 squares for each and positioning them 1 on top of the other as shown in figure B. Grasp and squeeze the center of the tissue layers to resemble a flower; set aside. Make 4 purple streamer flowers. To do this, wrap the streamer into a cone shape; then, wrap the streamer around the cone 10 or more times, securing the bottom edge with your fingers and tapering the upper edge out into a petal shape (figure C). Staple bottom edges together to secure; set aside. Gather up 1 sheet of green tissue paper crosswise to fit the headband; staple in place 1 in. from each edge. Starting at the center, position and staple a pink flower to the gathered tissue. Then, working out to each end, position and staple a purple flower and then another pink flower as shown in figure D. Carefully secure the gathered tissue (between the staples) to the headband, using a few small pieces of double-stick tape. Punch holes near the ends of the headband and tie closed to fit around the head of the wearer with a piece of round-cord elastic.

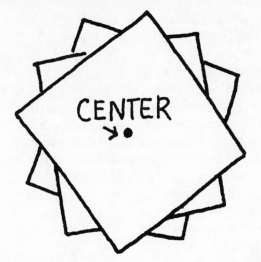

CENTER

SQUEEZE CENTER

FIGURE B

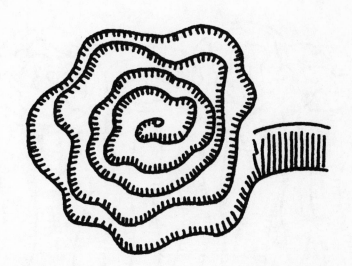

FIGURE C

FIGURE D

TO MAKE GRASS SKIRT: First make slashes in the waistband for weaving the "grass" through. To do this, work from the center out to each side. Using a craft knife, carefully cut a 2-in. slash ½ in. below the top waistband edge, then cut the next 2-in. slash ½ in. below the first and starting ⅝ in. in from the upper slash edge. By doing this, the upper grass pieces will partially overlap the ones below, creating a fuller look. End slashes 1½ in. in from band ends. There will be approximately 17 slashes. Using the 4 colors of streamer lengths, form the grass skirt by pulling 1 streamer approximately halfway through each slit, varying the colors as you go (figure E). Gather up 1 sheet of green tissue paper lengthwise to fit the waistband; staple in place 1 in. from each end. Starting at the center, position and staple 1 pink flower to the gathered tissue and then another halfway between the center and end on each side as shown in figure E. Carefully secure the gathered tissue to the waistband at the flower positions only, using a small piece of double-stick tape. Punch holes near the ends of the waistband and tie closed to fit around the wearer's waist or hips with a piece of round-cord elastic.

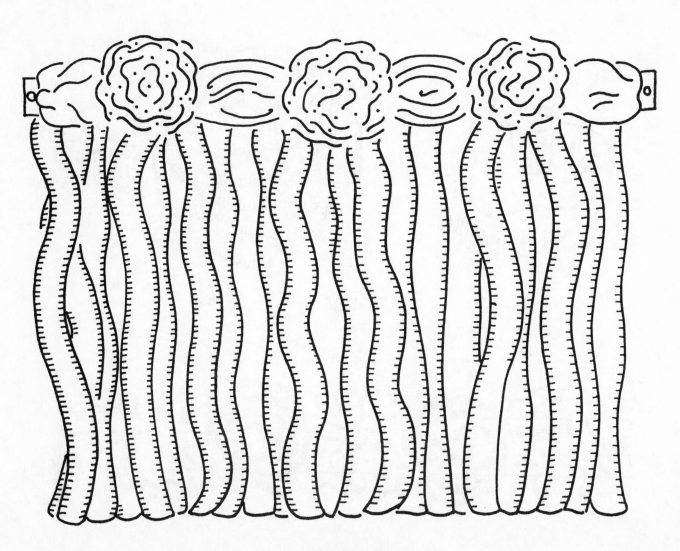

FIGURE E

TO MAKE THE LEI: Measure in 2 in. from the edge of the pink poster board circle all around and draw another circle, squaring off the sides slightly as shown in figure F; cut out inner circle to form a ring and cut across the ring at the top edge to form an opening. Gather, position, and staple 1 sheet of green tissue paper onto the ring, same as for the headband (figure G). Starting at the center and working out same as for the headband, staple pink and purple flowers to the gathered tissue. Cut approximately fifteen 2- to 2½-in. triangular leaf shapes from green crepe paper streamers. If desired, cut each leaf individually on a small piece of folded streamer, posi-tioning the leaf tip on the fold (this gives a double-leaf effect). Tuck 2 or 3 leaves under each flower as shown in figure G and secure to the tissue with small pieces of double-stick tape. Tape the tissue to the poster board ring under the flowers, same as for the grass skirt. Punch holes near the ends of the lei and tie closed with a piece of round-cord elastic.

ADULT SIZING: Widen the waistband to fit and lengthen the grass streamers.

SUGGESTIONS: Wear a coordinating bathing suit, leotard, or simple shirt with or without tights for the best effect.

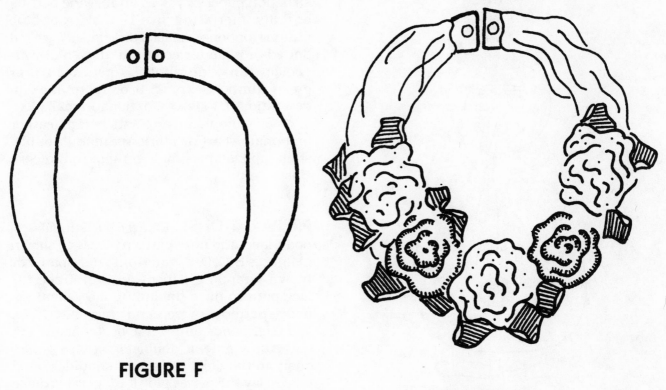

FIGURE F

FIGURE G

SNOWMAN

FIGURE A

This snowperson couldn't be much "cooler," parading around in his tropical shades! The face is attached to the hat for a very comfortable fit.

DESCRIPTION: Snow face/hatband and snowball slip-on body.

MATERIALS: 3 sheets of white and 1 sheet of black poster board; small pieces of yellow and orange poster board (preferably) or construction paper; 2 yds. of 45-in.-wide batting or fluffy interfacing; five 1-in. black or blue buttons (optional); black fabric tape; ½ yd. red dotted or plaid (or color and design of your choice) 1-in.-wide ribbon; 1 package red or green jumbo rickrack; 3 or more stick-on decorations for glasses (optional); small piece of green cellophane or plastic wrap; feather (optional); scarf or fabric remnant; double-stick tape; staples; hole punch; round-cord elastic; glue.

PREPARATIONS: Enlarge hat, sunglasses, body, face, and nose pattern pieces as shown in figures B, C, D, E, and F onto newspaper or brown wrapping paper; cut out. Trace the face pattern once (including face opening); body pattern twice, and two 2-×-12-in. shoulder bands onto white poster board; cut out. Apply glue or double-stick tape generously to the face, body, and shoulder band pieces; lay the pieces glue (or tape) side down on the batting and trim away excess along edges. Trace the hat and hat brim patterns onto black poster board, the sunglasses onto yellow poster board (or white poster board if using construction paper), and the nose patterns onto orange poster board (or white); cut out all pieces. (If using yellow and orange construction paper, trace and cut glasses pattern from yellow and nose patterns from orange; align and glue these pieces to the matching white poster board pieces.)

118

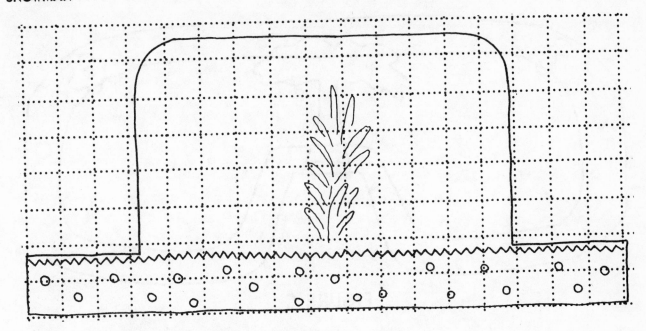

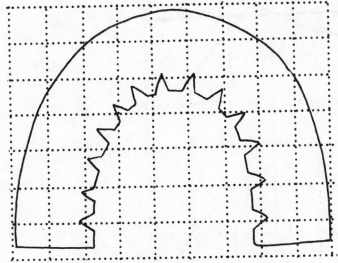

FIGURE B (1 sq. = 1 in.)

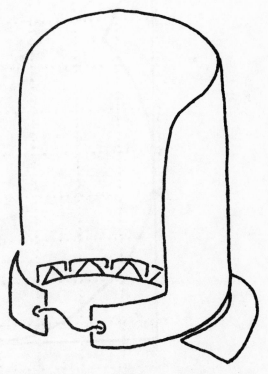

FIGURE E (1 sq. = 1½ in.)

TO MAKE HATBAND/FACE: Assemble the hat first, beginning by fitting the brim to the hat base. Bend the notched (inner) edge up on a 90-degree angle to the brim and place this edge along the inside lower edge of the hat, curving the hat to fit. Tape notches to hat as shown in figure G. To decorate hat, run a line of double-stick tape around the hat, 1 in. from each end and just above the brim; affix ribbon to tape, trimming ends as necessary. Punch holes near the ends of hatband and tie closed to fit around the head with a piece of round-cord elastic.

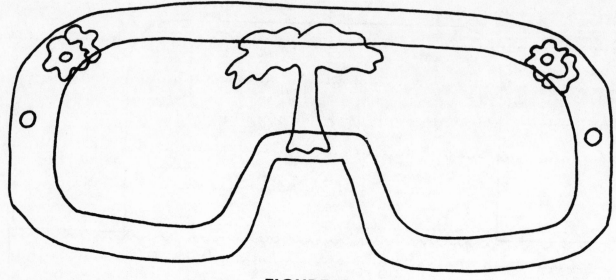

FIGURE C

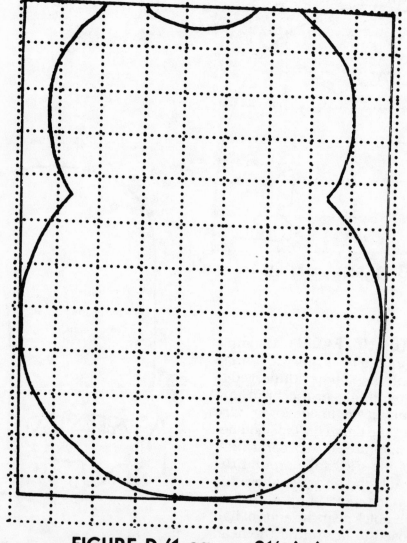

FIGURE D (1 sq. = 2½ in.)

Assemble the face pieces next, beginning with the nose. Fold nose base at tip as shown in figure H. Squeeze small beads of glue along one edge of nose base and affix upper nose piece in place; let dry (figure H). To assemble sunglasses, place small pieces of double-stick tape on the back side of the frame, and lay the frame, tape side down, onto a piece of cellophane or plastic wrap cut slightly larger than the frame. Trim the cellophane or wrap along the outside edge of the frame. Punch holes at the sides of the frame as indicated and tie a 14-in. piece of round-cord elastic through the holes to form a band (figure C). Decorate frame with stickers.

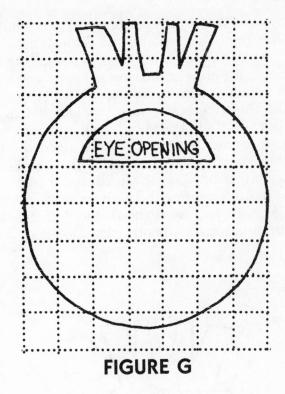

EYE OPENING

FIGURE G

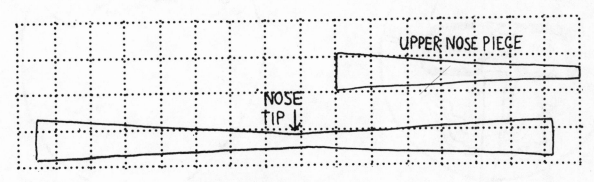

UPPER NOSE PIECE

NOSE TIP ↓

FIGURE F (1 sq. = 1 in.)

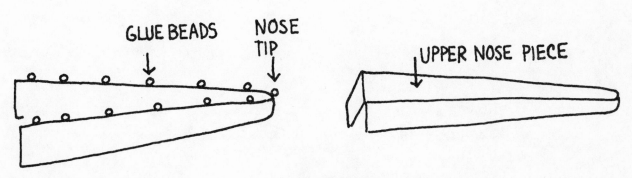

GLUE BEADS   NOSE TIP

UPPER NOSE PIECE

FIGURE H

To assemble the face, position and glue 2 button eyes (or 1-in. poster board circles) slightly below the face opening as shown in figure I. Fold in the ends at the base of the nose ¼ in. and position and glue to face; let dry. Position and glue rickrack mouth in place; let dry (figure I). Slide the sunglasses on over the head, tightening the elastic if needed. To attach face to hatband, place the notched face extension along the inside lower edge of the hat, centering the face; tape in place (figure J). Finish off the inside with black fabric tape for a smooth, clean look.

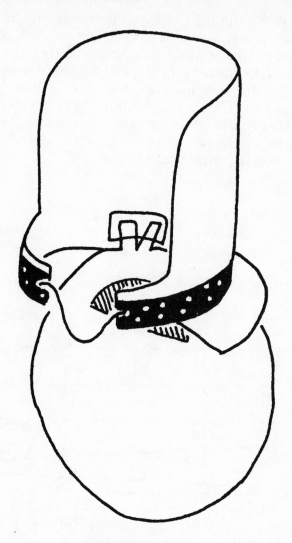

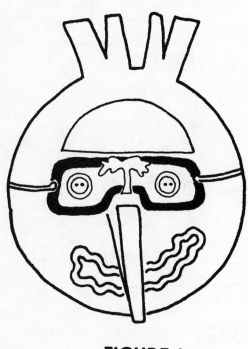

FIGURE I

FIGURE J

TO MAKE BODY: Position and glue 3 buttons (or 1-in. poster board circles) onto body front. Hold the front up to the wearer and mark the position of the shoulder edges onto the top edge; transfer these marks onto top edge of back body piece. Staple or tape ends of shoulder bands to wrong side of front and back body pieces at shoulder marks to fit as shown in figure K. Finish off costume with a scarf tied loosely around the neck.

ADULT SIZING: If necessary, enlarge facial opening to allow maximum visibility.

SUGGESTIONS: You can dress this ''person'' up to fit your fashion sense—change the color of the hat or decorate it with sequins . . .use your own sunglasses . . .put on a bow tie . . .add a polka-dot bikini!

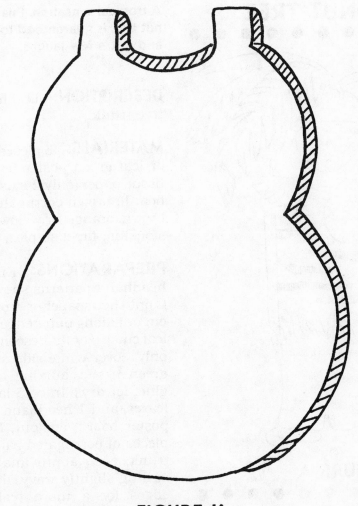

FIGURE K

CHAPTER V

BOTANICALS AND EDIBLES

COCONUT TREE

FIGURE A

A tropical sensation, this walking, talking coconut tree is guaranteed to raise a few eyebrows and get a few laughs.

DESCRIPTION: Leaf headband and slip-on tree trunk.

MATERIALS: 5 pieces of fluorescent green or leaf green poster board; 7 sheets green tissue paper (only 2 if using leaf green poster board); brown corrugated box cardboard; 1 brown, orange, or yellow balloon plus 1 dark stocking; tape; staples; glue; hole punch.

PREPARATIONS: Enlarge 2 leaf and headband patterns shown in figures B and C onto newspaper or brown wrapping paper; cut out along outer edges only (do not make leaf cuts). (For fluorescent green poster board only, cover white side of poster board with green tissue, affixing them together with glue; let dry.) Trace 5 large leaves, 3 small leaves, and 1 headband pattern onto green poster board; cut out. Measure and cut 2 pieces of corrugated cardboard for the tree trunk, each approximately 14 × 26 in.—cutting slightly wavy along the lengthwise edges for a more realistic look—and 2 shoulder bands, 2 × 12 in.

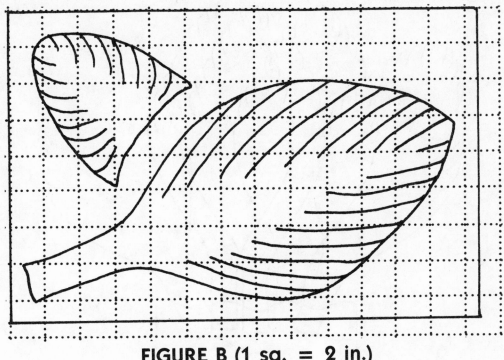

FIGURE B (1 sq. = 2 in.)

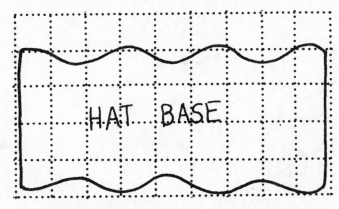

HAT BASE

FIGURE C (1 sq. = 1¾ in.)

TO MAKE HEADBAND: For each large leaf, gently fold in half lengthwise just enough to make a slight crease in the poster board. Then, beginning at the leaf tip, make leaf cuts on each side of the crease as shown in figure B. Fold the headband in half, so scalloped edges meet; finger-crease, then open up again. Fold 1 sheet of tissue paper crosswise 2 times and gather it up along one edge to fit on the wrong side of the headband as shown in figure D; tape in place. Position 5 large leaves, wrong side up (if tissue-covered) onto wrong side of headband as shown; staple in place (figure D). Refold the headband and staple together at both ends. Punch holes near the ends and tie closed to fit around the head with a piece of round-cord elastic (figure E). When worn, the leaves will gently fold over the band as shown in figure A.

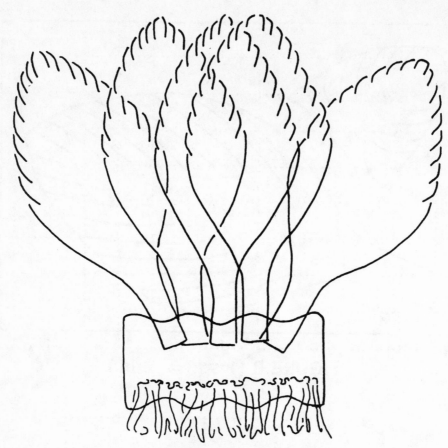

FIGURE D

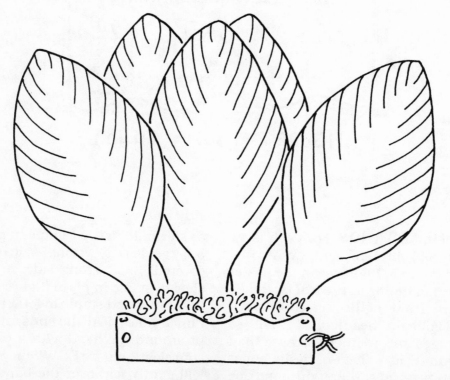

FIGURE E

TO MAKE TREE TRUNK:

First create the bark texture. To do this, peel strips of the top paper layer from the corrugated cardboard trunk, starting from the side edge as shown in figure F. Then, join the front and back together. Hold the front up to the wearer and mark the position of the shoulder edges on inner top edge; transfer these marks to wrong side of back top edges. Staple the ends of each shoulder band to wrong side of the front and back at shoulder marks to fit. Crease and cut the small leaves, same as for headband leaves. Cut 1 leaf along crease to form 2 halves. Staple these leaves to front neck edge as shown in figure F. To make the coconut, blow the brown balloon up until slightly full and staple end under the small coconut leaves. If using orange or yellow balloon carefully pull a stocking over it; twist the excess of the stocking at both ends, join them together at the knotted end of the balloon, and staple together. Trim away all but 1 in. of the stocking ends and inconspicuously staple to tree trunk so coconut hangs out from under the leaves (figure A). To complete the trunk, gather up a sheet of green tissue or cut a piece of poster board to fit the lower edge of trunk, glue at bottom, and let dry; grass-cut gathered tissue or poster board as shown in figure F.

ADULT SIZING:

If desired, you can lengthen the tree trunk.

SUGGESTIONS:

For ease in sitting, the back trunk can be made shorter, so that it ends at the waist. For a small child, 3 headband leaves would be sufficient.

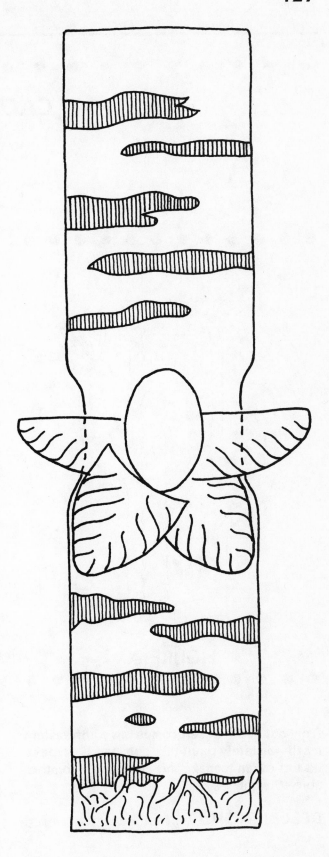

FIGURE F

CACTUS

FIGURE A

From out of the desert comes this southwestern motif—a stately plant that commands respect. It's lots of fun to make and deceivingly comfortable to wear.

DESCRIPTION: One-piece felt-covered cactus.

MATERIALS: ⅔ yd. light green 72-in.-wide felt; 2 pieces green poster board; 8 yds. strung

green sequins; 18-×-24-in. piece of corrugated box cardboard; 1 square of red, yellow, or pink felt, or small pieces of red and yellow cellophane wrap, or netting for the flower (optional); glue; staples; craft knife (optional); hole punch; round-cord elastic or ¼-in. elastic.

PREPARATIONS: Enlarge cactus pattern in figure B onto newspaper or brown wrapping paper; cut out. Open up the felt and lay out flat; pin cactus pattern to felt as shown and cut out. Cut a 2½-in. band from the top edge of 1 piece of poster board as shown in figure C. Join 2 pieces of poster board together, overlapping slightly as shown in figure C, and tape securely together.

TO MAKE CACTUS: Using a thin layer of glue along the felt edges, secure the upper portion of cactus to poster board as shown in figure C; let dry. Cut the face hole 4¾ in. from the top of the cactus and attach the headband to the wrong side, stapling near the center of the face opening as shown. Working with cactus right side up (felt up), draw straight glue lines, 6 to 12 in. at a time, following the line patterns in figure D, and lay on strung sequins, string side down; let dry. Trace the midsection of the cactus (arms included) onto the corrugated board. Cut out carefully with a craft knife or scissors. Punch 4 holes in the board 1 in. from the top and bottom edges as shown. Tie 2 pieces of elastic diagonally across the board to fit across the back of the wearer as shown. Then, draw a glue line along the inside edges and affix the board to the wrong side of the cactus as shown in figure E; let dry. Punch holes near the ends of the headband and tie closed to fit around the wearer's head with a piece of round-cord elastic. The head closure serves merely to hold the cactus top in place; the support for the costume comes from the elastic cross straps.

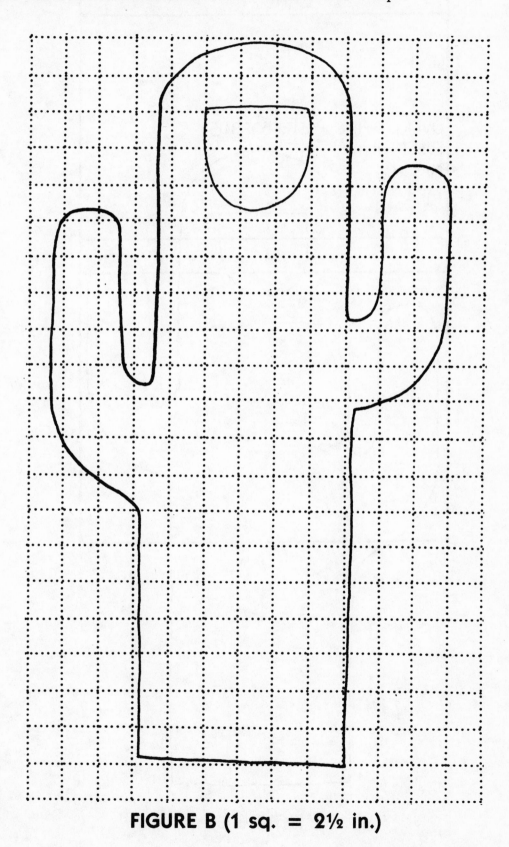

FIGURE B (1 sq. = 2½ in.)

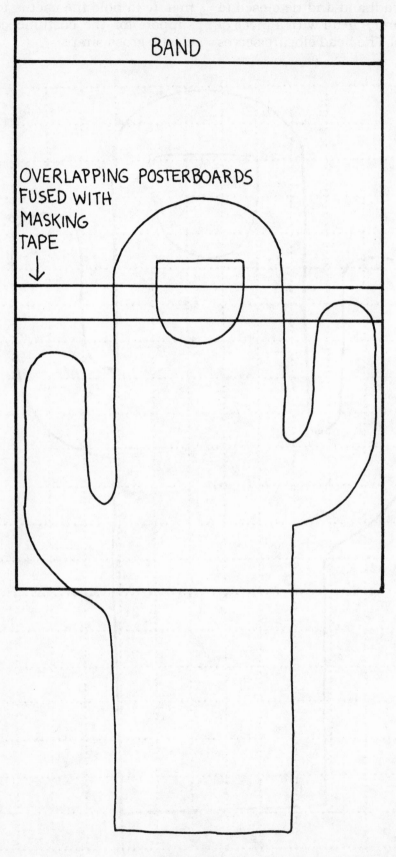

FIGURE C

TO ADD CACTUS FLOWERS (optional):

Make a few layers of small felt, cellophane, or netting squares, and gather the squares up from the center, securing them together with a staple, string, or rubber band. Position on cactus as desired and staple or glue in place.

ADULT SIZING: No alterations necessary, although you can lengthen the cactus if you wish.

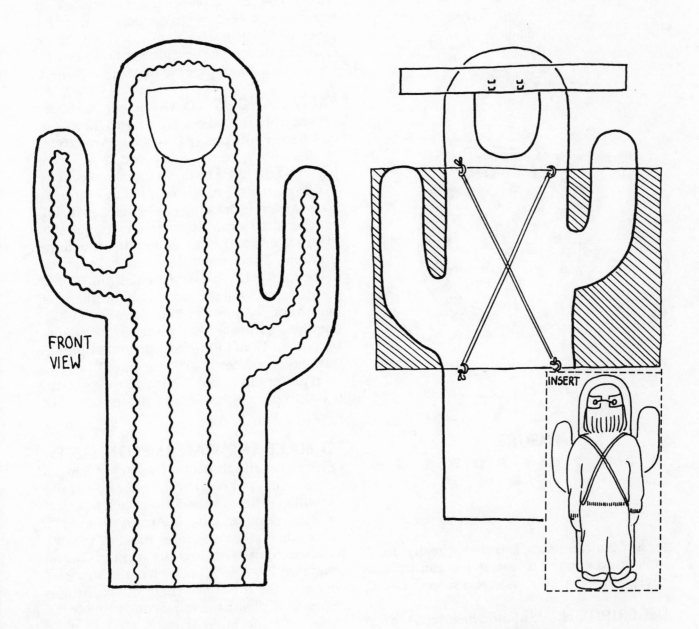

FRONT VIEW

INSERT

FIGURE D

FIGURE E

WATERMELON

FIGURE A

Fresh from the patch, this melon really does look good enough to eat. If you can trace a circle, you'll find this costume a snap to make.

DESCRIPTION: Leaf-top headband and slip-on watermelon slice.

MATERIALS: 2 pieces each of white and red and 4 pieces of green poster board; 1 piece of black poster board or 1 yd. black Con-Tact paper; staples; glue or double-stick tape; 1 or 2 green pipe cleaners; hole punch.

PREPARATIONS: Draw and cut two 20-in. circles from red poster board, two 22-in. circles from white poster board, and two 26-in. circles from green poster board (2 pieces of poster board must be taped together securely to accommodate each of these large circles). To make circle drawing easier, use a pail, lid, or other large round object that is comparable in size to one of the circles, and use it to draw that one. Then, draw the remaining circles accordingly. Or, make a pencil and string compass, making the string half the diameter (width) of each circle. Trace two 2-×-14-in. shoulder bands, a 2-×-16-in. headband (optional), and leaf (optional) shown in figure B onto green poster board; cut out. Trace the seed pattern in figure C 20 to 40 times or cut it out freehand from black poster board or Con-Tact paper.

TO MAKE THE WATERMELON SLICE: Center and attach each of the white circles to the green and each of the red circles onto the white, using glue or double-stick tape and creating a front and back. Arrange the seeds randomly on the red circles and glue or stick in place (figure D). Hold the front up to the wearer and mark the position of the shoulder edges on the top inner edge; transfer these marks to the back top inner edges. Staple the shoulder band ends at the front and back shoulder marks to fit as shown in figure D.

132

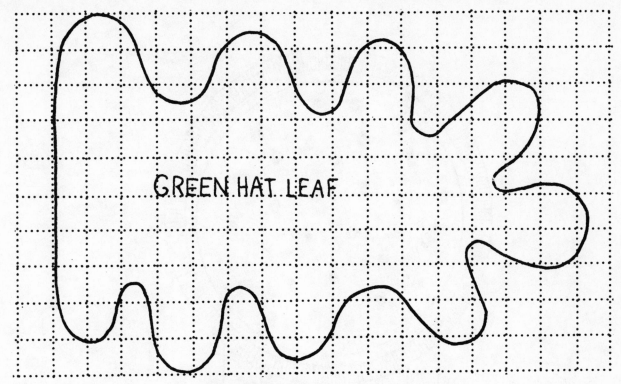

GREEN HAT LEAF

FIGURE B (1 sq. = 1 in.)

FIGURE C

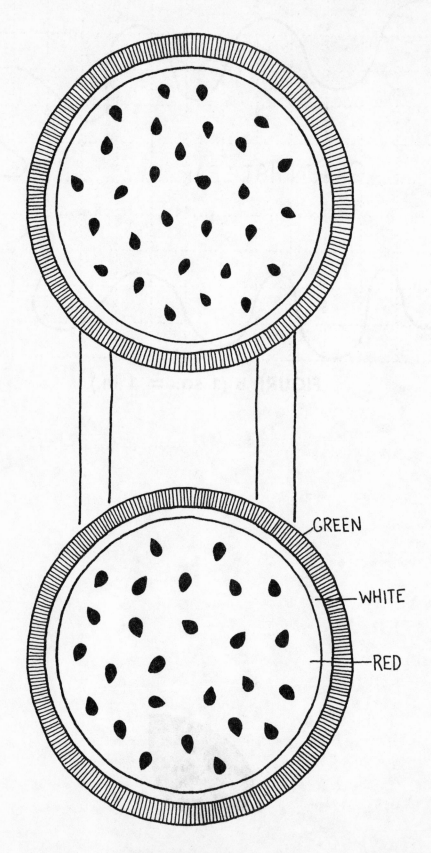

FIGURE D

TO MAKE THE HEADBAND (optional):

Punch holes near the ends of the headband and tie closed to fit around the head with a piece of round-cord elastic. Mark the position just above one ear on the headband, remove, and staple the leaf end in place on this mark as shown (figure E). Punch a hole close to stapled leaf edge, push a bit of pipe cleaner through to the wrong side to secure, and coil the rest as shown.

ADULT SIZING: No alterations necessary.

SUGGESTIONS: Simple green or black clothing is most effective with this costume—tights and a leotard or turtleneck are ideal.

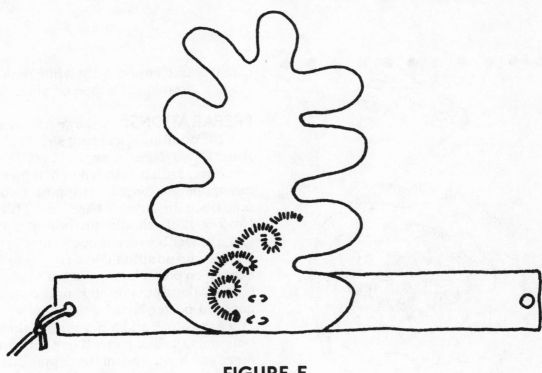

FIGURE E

SALAD

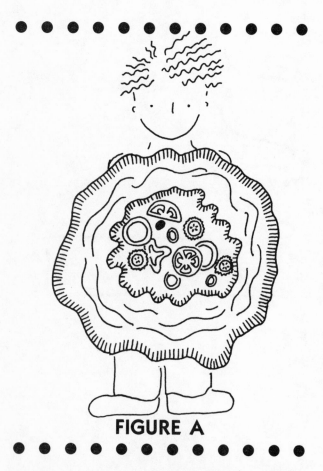

FIGURE A

A gardener's delight, this freshly tossed green salad is all the dressing you'll need (see illustration on front cover).

DESCRIPTION: Slip-on tossed salad.

MATERIALS: 2 pieces medium green and 1 piece each of fluorescent or bright green and fluorescent or bright red poster board; roll of green cellophane wrapping paper; ¼ yd. each green and red Con-Tact paper; small piece of yellow and black Con-Tact paper or

construction paper; plain white paper; tape; staples; double-stick tape or glue.

PREPARATIONS: Enlarge 2 lettuce leaves and the additional leaf ring shown in figures B and C and trace the tomato, pepper, cucumber, olive, radish, and onion in figure D onto newspaper or brown wrapping paper; cut out. Trace the larger, "base" leaf 2 times and two 2-×-12-in. shoulder bands onto medium green poster board; cut out. Trace the smaller lettuce and additional leaf ring onto fluorescent green poster board; cut out. Trace tomato pattern along outside edge only onto fluorescent red poster board 3 or 4 times; cut out. Trace the outer and inner lines of the tomato onto red Con-Tact paper 3 or 4 times and the outer and inner lines of the pepper onto green and yellow Con-Tact paper 2 times each; cut all pieces out. Trace 5 or 6 radishes from red Con-Tact paper, 5 or 6 cucumbers from green, 5 olives from black, and 6 or 7 onion rings from white paper; cut out.

Make the vegetables. For each tomato, align and adhere the Con-Tact paper tomato piece to the poster board tomato, trimming if necessary; cut tiny seeds from red Con-Tact paper and secure on poster board section of tomato. For each cucumber, cut an inner circle from the green Con-Tact paper, approximately ¼ in. from the edge, forming a ring; stick ring onto a piece of white paper that is slightly larger than the ring, and trim away excess along outer green edge. Cut 4 to 6 small seeds from green Con-Tact paper and stick on cucumber as shown. Treat radishes same as cucumbers, forming a ring that sticks on white paper and is trimmed.

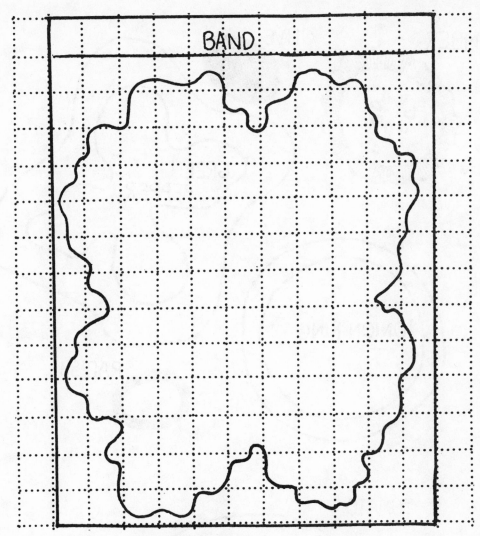

FIGURE B (1 sq. = 2 in.)

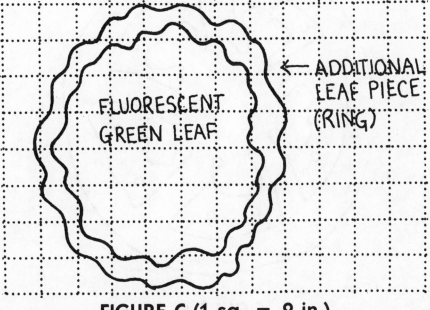

FIGURE C (1 sq. = 2 in.)

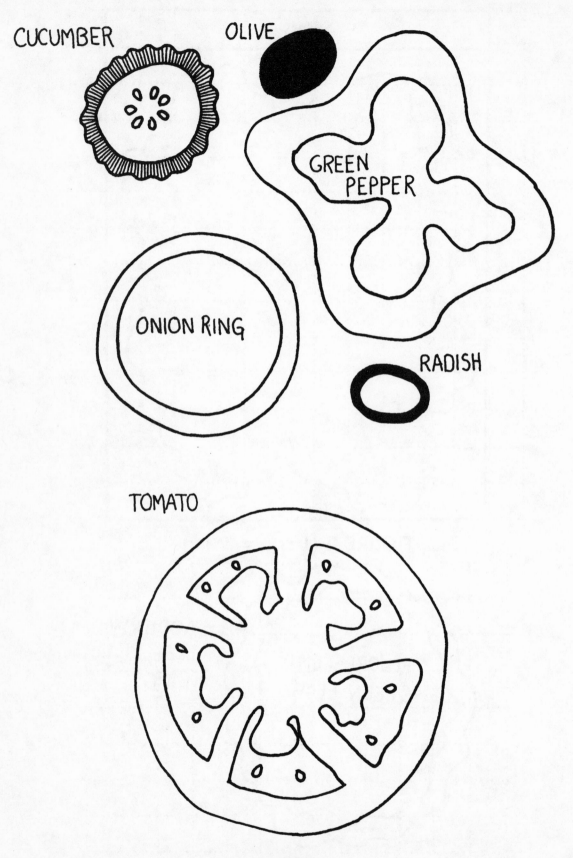

FIGURE D

TO MAKE THE SALAD: Lay 1 of the large lettuce leaves on a flat surface. Unroll the green cellophane and fold it lengthwise, not quite in half, finger-creasing the folded edge. Beginning a few inches from the center of the lettuce leaf and working around in a circle, gather and tape the creased cellophane edge to form a double layer of lettuce on top of the poster board lettuce (figure E). Arrange the tomatoes, green and yellow peppers, cucumbers, radishes, olives, and onion rings onto the fluorescent green leaf as shown in figure E. Secure with small pieces of double-stick tape or glue (stick on the peppers). Center the vegetable-topped leaf on top of the cellophane lettuce and secure well with double-stick tape. Tuck the extra lettuce ring between the 2 layers of cellophane lettuce to give the illusion of an additional layer of lettuce; tape inconspicuously. Hold the completed salad front up to the wearer and mark the position of the shoulders on the inner top edges; transfer these marks to the inner top edges of the back leaf. Staple the ends of the shoulder bands at the marks on the front and back to fit as shown in figure E.

ADULT SIZING: No alterations necessary.

SUGGESTIONS: Dressing in green complements this delicious salad.

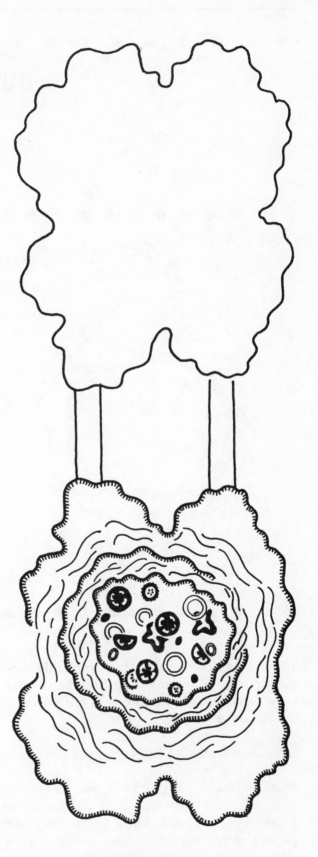

FIGURE E

BURGER

FIGURE A

This burger comes with the works—lettuce, tomato, and a sesame-seed bun! The burger meat sandwiched in between is the wearer of the disguise.

DESCRIPTION: Slip-on burger fixings.

MATERIALS: ½ yd. tan, ¼ yd. green, and ⅛ yd. red 72-in.-wide felt; 2 pieces tan or brown poster board; small bag of polyester filling; gold sequins; glue; straight pins; staples; tape.

PREPARATIONS: Measure and cut 3 oval pattern pieces—1 (the bun top) 20 × 24 in., the second 1 in. smaller all around than the first, and the third 1 in. smaller all around than the second—from newspaper or brown paper; cut out. Following the layout in figure B, pin the largest oval pattern onto folded tan felt and cut out. Trace the second oval 3 times and the third (smallest) oval 2 times and two 2-×-12-in. shoulder bands from tan or brown poster board; cut out. Cut the green felt in half lengthwise, forming 2 strips, each 4½ × 72 in.

TO MAKE BURGER: For top bun half, lay tan or brown bun felt out flat and cover with polyester filling, leaving outer felt edge uncovered approximately 1 in. all around. Make the filling deeper in the middle, tapering out to the edges to form a typical bun shape. Place 1 of the second ovals over the filling, centering it over the felt. Working on a small section at a time, squeeze a thin line of glue ½ in. from the poster board edge, fold 1 in. felt edge over onto the poster board, gathering as needed, and finger-press to adhere. Pin felt edge to poster board if necessary to hold in place; continue all the way around, let dry, then remove pins (figure C). To add the tomato, fold the red felt in half lengthwise and position it with raw edges in and folded edge extending beyond the outer bun edge by 1 in. or more. Glue, position, and pin a small section at a time, same as for bun edge (figure D); overlap slightly where the ends meet and trim. Let dry and remove pins. Add the green felt lettuce leaf (not folded), same as for tomato, gathering the inner leaf edge as you

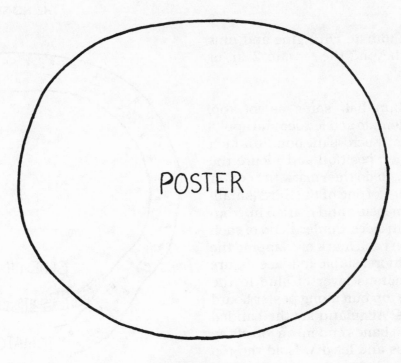

FIGURE B

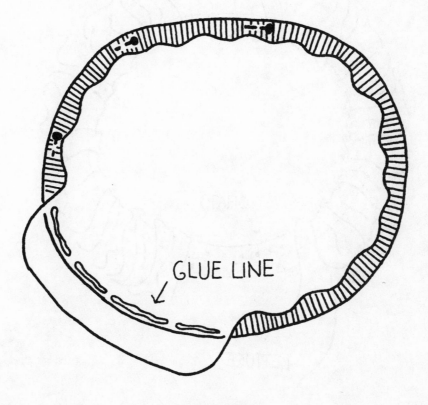

FIGURE C

secure it to the tomato with glue and pins and extending beyond the tomato 2 in. or more (figure E).

Make bottom bun half same as for top, eliminating the tomato and lettuce and applying the filling evenly across the bun. To attach the buns together, position and secure the shoulder bands. To do this, mark the center along the top edge of one of the third (smallest) ovals, then measure and mark 5 in. from the center on both sides. Center 1 end of each shoulder band on each mark overlapping the oval by 1 in. or more; staple in place (figure F). Apply a generous layer of glue to the underside of the top bun along poster board at the leaf edges. Align and lay the banded oval (with stapled bands end in) on top of the glue; finger-press and let dry. Hold the top and bottom bun halves up to the wearer, and tape the remaining band ends to the inner edge of the bottom (back) bun to fit; remove.

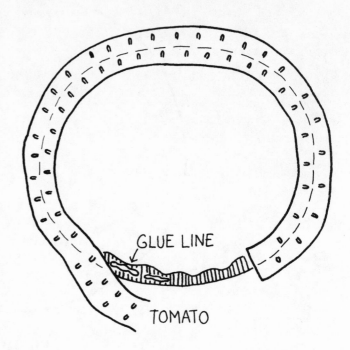

FIGURE D

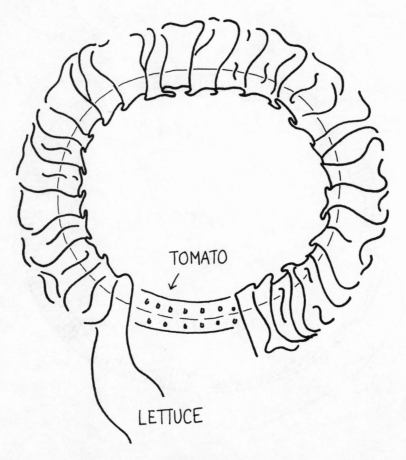

FIGURE E

Apply a generous layer of glue to the poster board on the bottom bun, and align and lay the remaining oval on top of the glue, same as for top. Let dry.

To finish off bun, add the sequin sesame seeds, arranging small drops of glue and applying sequins as shown in figure F.

ADULT SIZING: No alterations are necessary.

SUGGESTIONS: Since the wearer is the burger in this costume, brown clothing is preferable but not essential.

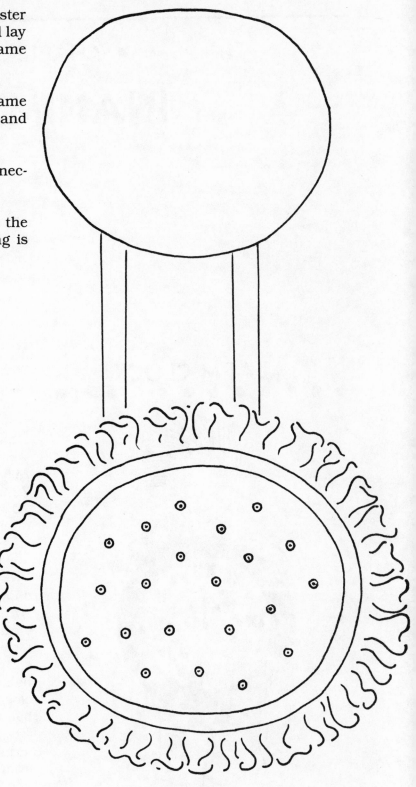

FIGURE F

● ● ● CHAPTER VI ● ● ●

INANIMATES

ALARM CLOCK

FIGURE A

This elegant timepiece is right on the number for good looks and easy wearability (see illustration on front cover).

DESCRIPTION: Slip-on alarm clock.

MATERIALS: ¾ yd. black and ⅔ yd. white 72-in.-wide felt; 4 yds. strung gold sequins; 20 MM flat black sequins (optional); 1 piece of black poster board; glue; gold glitter and loose sequins.

PREPARATIONS: Enlarge clock pattern shown in figure B onto newspaper or brown wrapping paper; cut out. Make a 19-in. circle and trace the letters and clock-hand patterns in figure C onto newspaper or brown wrapping paper; cut out and fold circle in half. Following the layout in figure B, pin the clock pattern on the folded black felt and the half-circle pattern on the folded white felt; cut out. Using the number and clock-hand patterns, cut 17 I's, 5 V's, 4 X's, and 2 hands from black felt. Trim 1 in. from end of 1 clock hand to make the shorter hand as shown.

TO MAKE CLOCK: Lay white circle flat. This will be the face of the clock. Arrange the numerals around the edge of the face, evenly

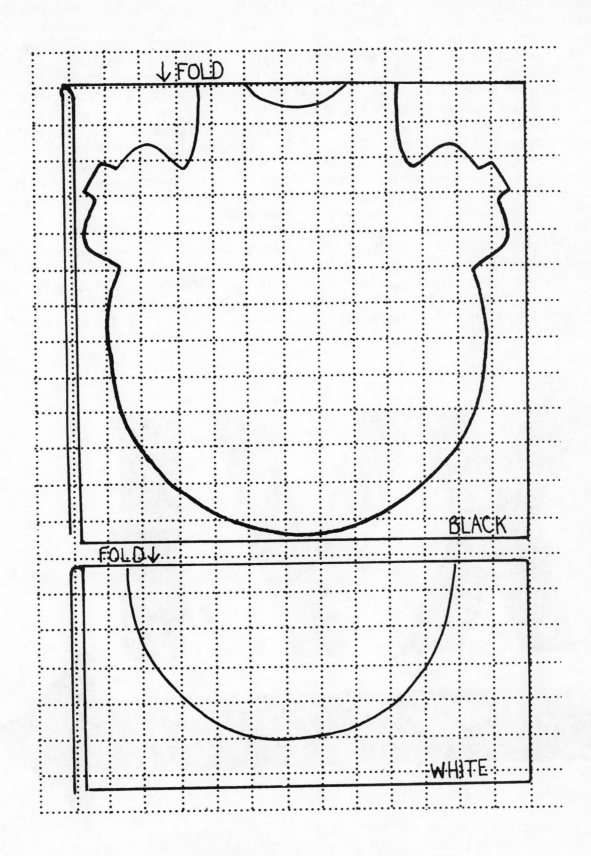

↓FOLD

BLACK

FOLD↓

WHITE

FIGURE B (1 sq. = 2 in.)

spaced and in proper sequence; glue in place (figure E). Lay the 12-hour dots—the flat black sequins—next to the numerals (optional); glue in place. Lay the hands on to read 11:55 as shown; glue in place. Cover the center where the clock hand ends intersect with a flat black sequin; glue and let dry. Lay the black felt clock base out flat. Trim off 1 set of bells to create the back side, and cut a 4-in. slit at the center back neck edge as shown in figure D. Cut a 12-in.-wide scoop to a depth of 2 in. from the center of a piece of 10-×-24-in. black poster board. Slide the poster board under the clock base, below the neck, making sure the bell caps are completely on the poster board. (The center of the scoop will be 4 in. below the center of the neckline.) Glue the felt to the poster board and trim to the edge of the felt (figure D). Lay the clock face on the front of the clock base (side with bells),

1½ in. from the bottom edge; center and glue in place. Draw a thin line of glue onto clock base, along the edge of the face; lay the strung sequins, string side down, onto the glue, encircling the face 2 times. Press down carefully and allow to dry. Cover 1 bell portion at a time with a layer of glue and cover with a mixture of gold glitter and loose gold sequins; let dry (figure E). Try not to use too generous an amount of glue for this process, as it may cause the poster board to warp. Try the clock on the wearer, and lengthen back slit if necessary to fit over the head.

ADULT SIZING: No alterations necessary.

SUGGESTIONS: The use of black and white with gold accents gives a sharp, clean look to this clock. It can, however, be made in the colors of your choice.

FIGURE C

ALARM CLOCK

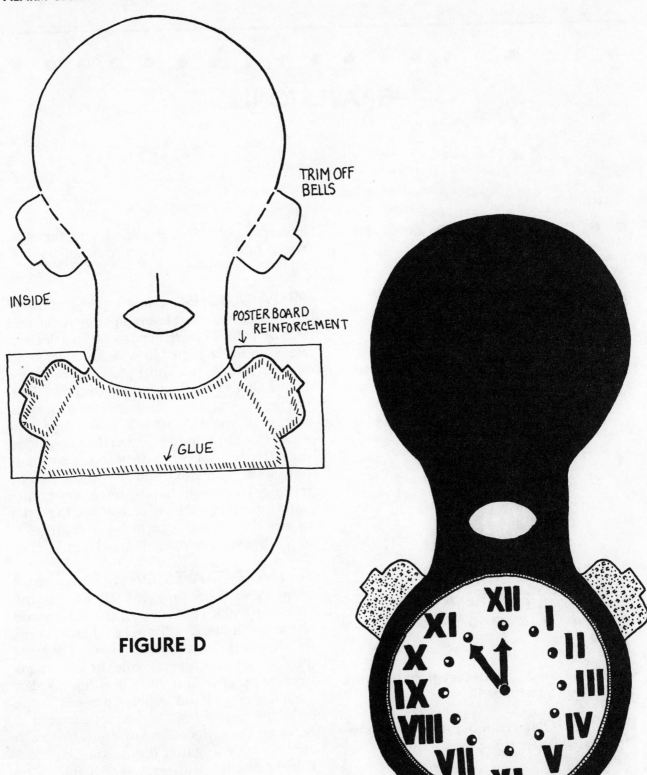

TRIM OFF
BELLS

INSIDE

POSTER BOARD
REINFORCEMENT

GLUE

FIGURE D

FIGURE E

GRAVESTONE

FIGURE A

Beware the deadly hands that grasp the gravestone. What's to follow?!!

DESCRIPTION: Humorous slip-on gravestone with flowers.

MATERIALS: 2 pieces of black poster board; stainless steel, silver, or gray and black acrylic paints; 2 sheets each of white, pink, and red tissue or crepe paper; small piece of green poster board (or white, plus a green marker) for flower stems; heavy white paper;

small piece of red paper; clean kitchen sponge; small paintbrush or cotton swab; double-stick tape; staples.

PREPARATIONS: Using a sponge and gray acrylic paint, completely sponge-print one side of 2 black pieces of poster board; let dry. Measure and mark a 2-in.-wide shoulder strap as shown in figure B on 1 piece of the poster board. On the remainder, draw the gravestone shape by simply rounding the corners as shown (figure B); cut out gravestone and strap. Cut strap in half. Trace the gravestone onto the second piece of poster board; cut out. Make 1 or more left and right hands, tracing your own hands on heavy white paper, including 2 in. of arm above the wrist (figure C); cut out. Cut out 4 to 6 strips of green poster board, each ¼ ×16 in.

TO MAKE GRAVESTONE: With a small paintbrush or cotton swab, letter the gravestone in black paint, using the inscription shown in figure E—"Here lies Justin Time, beloved father of Noah Moore, RIP"—or another of your choice. While the lettering is drying, make a limp bunch of flowers. For each flower, roll and bunch a piece of tissue or crepe paper together and sandwich it between the ends of one of the ¼-in. green strips; staple together (figure D). Tie 4 to 6 flowers together with string and staple to the bottom of the gravestone front (figure E). Position and adhere hands, using double-stick tape, onto upper gravestone front, trimming excess hand and arm parts at the edge. From red paper, cut ten 3-in. fingernails to fit hands; adhere. Note that the appearance of

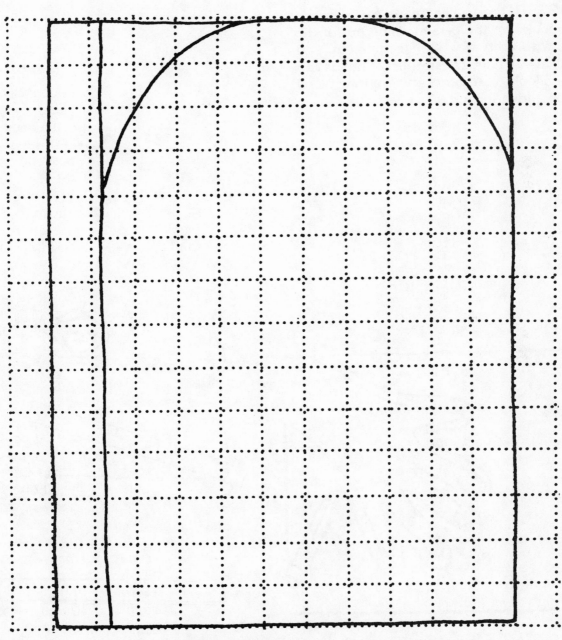

FIGURE B (1 sq. = 2 in.)

the thumbnails may vary depending on the position of the thumbs.

Hold the front up to the wearer and mark the position of the shoulder edges on the inner top edge; transfer these marks to the inner top edge of the back. Staple the shoulder band ends to the front and back at the marks to fit.

ADULT SIZING: No alterations are necessary.

SUGGESTIONS: The wearer can be made up to look like the person rising out of the grave with a bit of white face makeup and white, messy hair. The number of hands can vary—5 look great. Scars and dripping blood can be added for a gorier effect.

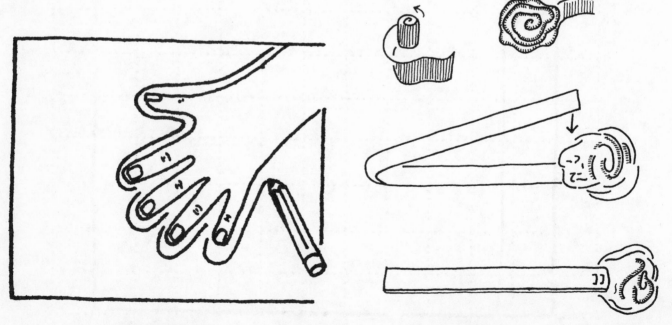

FIGURE C   **FIGURE D**

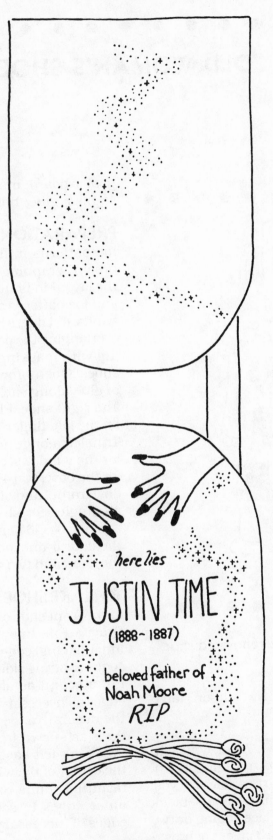

FIGURE E

OLD WOMAN'S SHOE

FIGURE A

Move into the old woman's renovated shoe—it's comfortable living!

DESCRIPTION: Decorative slip-on fairy-tale shoe.

MATERIALS: 1 yd. brown 72-in.-wide felt; 1 square each of dark brown, light brown, pink, yellow, white, and green felt; 1¼ yds. brown or black strung sequins; 5 yds. black lacing cord; ½ yd. of 2¼-in. lace edging or two 4-in.-square lace remnants; 3 pieces of brown poster board; masking or other strong tape; staples; glue; hole punch.

PREPARATIONS: Enlarge the boot and toe patterns in figure B onto newspaper or brown wrapping paper; cut out. Following the layout in figure B, trace 2 each of the boot and toe patterns and two 3-×-15-in. shoulder bands; cut out. Align and attach toes to boots, overlapping the poster board edges and securing with masking tape (figure B), to create 2 shoes. Open brown felt out flat. Draw a line of glue along each shoe edge, creating a left and right shoe. Place shoes, glue side down, on the felt, finger-press to secure, and let dry. Trim felt along shoe edges. Using felt squares for the windows, cut two 4¾-in. pink squares for the base, two 4¾-in. white squares for window frame, and six 1½-×-4¾-in. light brown rectangles for shutters and window boxes. Cut one 4-×-6¼-in. light brown rectangle for the door frame, one 3½-×-6-in. rectangle for the door, and two 4-in. lengths of lace edging.

TO MAKE SHOE: You will be adding details to the front shoe only. Set aside second shoe. Draw a thin line of glue 2½ in. in from the inner (lacing) edge of the shoe and lay strung sequins, string side down, onto the glue (forming a seam) as shown in figure C; trim at edges as necessary. Repeat this procedure for the decorative toe seam. Next, create 2 windows as shown in figure D. Lay lace edging over pink felt base. Cut a 3-in. square from the center of the white felt square and lay the resulting frame on top of lace. Glue along inner edges to secure (figure D) and trim edges if necessary. Position windows and

152

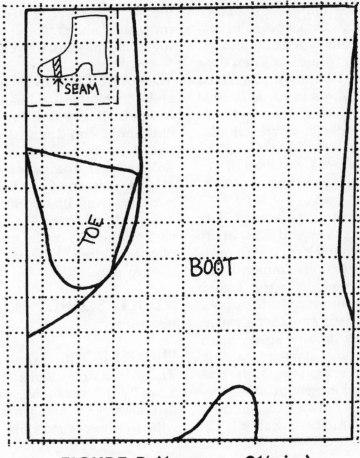

FIGURE B (1 sq. = 2½ in.)

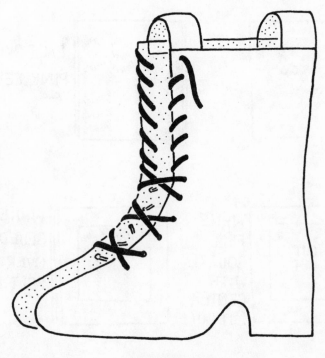

FIGURE C

brown felt window boxes onto shoe as shown in figure E, and glue in place; position and glue shutters along side edges of windows. Position and glue door frame and then door in place on shoe (figure E). Make multicolored tulips and circular flowers (¼-in. felt circle glued on ⅝-in. felt circle) as shown in figure F. Glue tulips along sides of door and circular flowers on top edge of window boxes as shown in figure E. If desired, add a small, circular felt doorknob and heart on the door.

Make lacing holes on front shoe, using a hole punch, 1 in. from the edge and 2 in. apart (figures E and G). Align back shoe with front and mark placement of holes; punch holes where marked. Hold shoe up to the wearer and mark shoulder position on inside upper edge. Staple 1 end of each shoulder strap at mark. Hold shoe up to wearer again, align back shoe with front, and staple remaining strap ends to back shoe. Beginning at the bottom, lace shoes together loosely, up to slightly above wearer's waist. Continue threading 1 lace only up the front and the other only up the back as shown (figure G) to leave room

for the wearer's arms. (For tiny children, lace individual shoes all the way up, rather than together, for easy movement.)

TO MAKE CHILDREN (optional): Trace children, clothes, and hair patterns as shown in figure H; cut out. Pin and cut 2 each of children 1 and 2, and 1 each of children 3 and 4 (or more or less according to your preferences) from white felt. Pin and cut clothes patterns from colored felt and hair patterns from black, brown, or yellow felt. Assemble children by lightly gluing their clothes and hair on; let dry. Arrange the completed children in logical places on the shoe; glue to shoe.

ADULT SIZING: No alterations are necessary.

SUGGESTION: To add a bit of humor, the wearer can dress like an old woman. Or, for a totally different look, eliminate all details (windows, door, lacing) and decorate the shoe with sequins to look like a western boot.

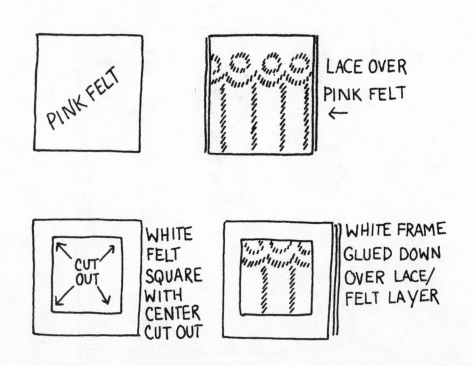

FIGURE D

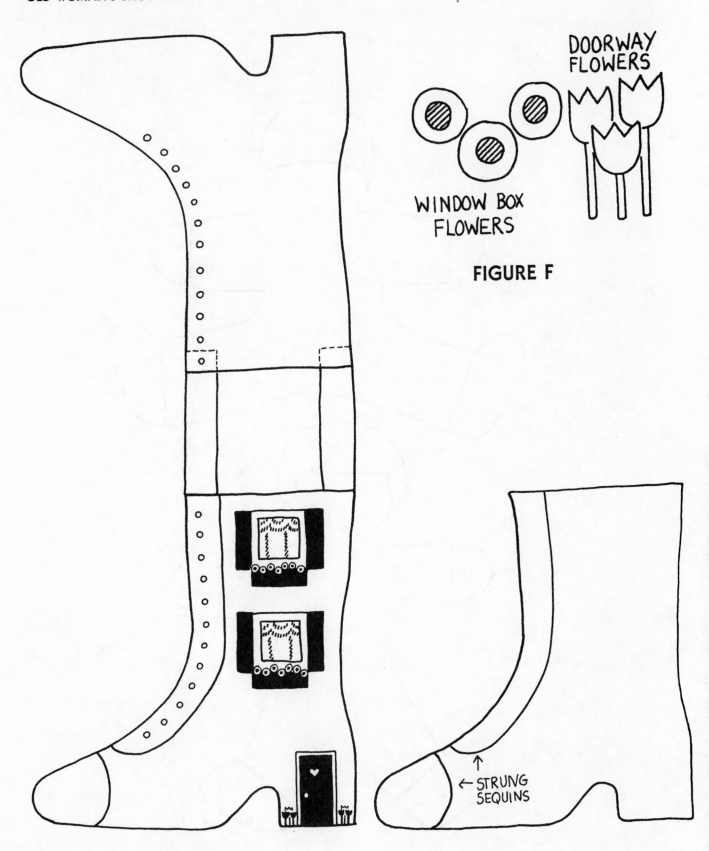

DOORWAY
FLOWERS

WINDOW BOX
FLOWERS

FIGURE F

← STRUNG
SEQUINS

FIGURE E

FIGURE G

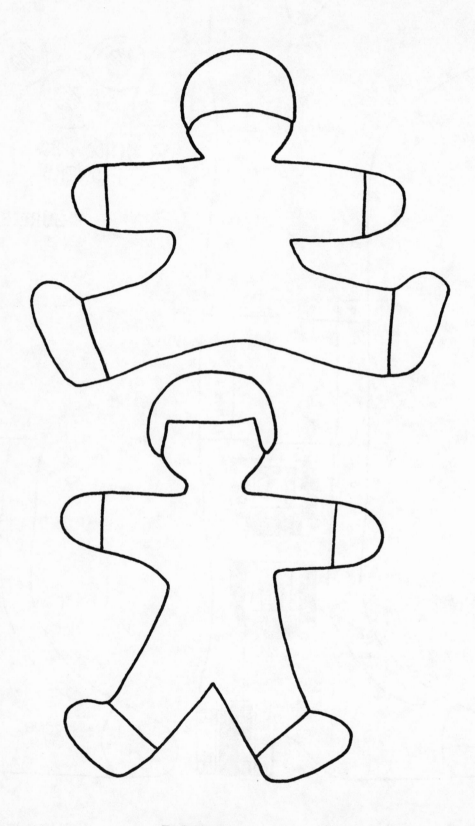

FIGURE H

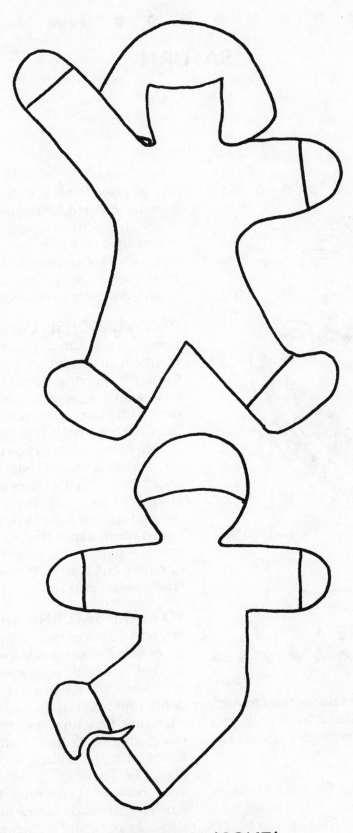

FIGURE H (CONT.)

SATURN

FIGURE A

A cosmic wonder, planet Saturn comes to earth in all its splendor. Encircled by 7 rings, this costume is amazingly comfortable to wear and easy to get around in.

DESCRIPTION: Slip-on Saturn with rings.

MATERIALS: 4 pieces of black poster board; stainless steel, silver, or gray acrylic paint; 4⅔ yds. each of 3 different iridescent or metallic-colored strung sequins; blue and/or deep pink glitter (optional); ¼ yd. each of yellow and violet (or 2 colors of choice) felt, or comparable amount of paper; two 20-in.-square or larger pieces of corrugated cardboard; tape; double-stick tape; glue; staples.

PREPARATIONS: Cut two 20-in.-diameter circles from black poster board and two identical circles from corrugated cardboard. Completely sponge-paint black poster-board circles on 1 side with acrylic paint. Lightly dust with glitter while paint is wet (optional). Enlarge ring-structure pattern shown in figure B onto newspaper or brown wrapping paper; cut out along outside edges only. Trace ring-structure pattern 2 times and two 2-×-12-in. shoulder bands onto black poster board; cut out along outside lines only. Cut ring-structure pattern along ring #1 and #3 lines. Pin or trace pattern for ring #1 onto yellow felt or paper; cut 4 rings. Pin or trace pattern for ring #3 onto purple felt or paper; cut 4 rings.

TO MAKE SATURN: Trim away the outer straight edges of each black ring structure, ¾ ×4⅜ in. on each side, as shown in figure C. Then, slash the midsection, cutting on the solid lines; the slashes must be cut the same depth (approximately ¾ in.). On each side of each ring structure, secure rings #1 and #3, using dots of glue or double-stick tape for paper, and positioning same as for pattern (figure B). There will be a ring of black poster board between the felt rings. Draw a thin line of glue along the center of the black ring (dividing it into 2 rings), and lay strung sequins, string side down, on the glue (figure D); trim.

158

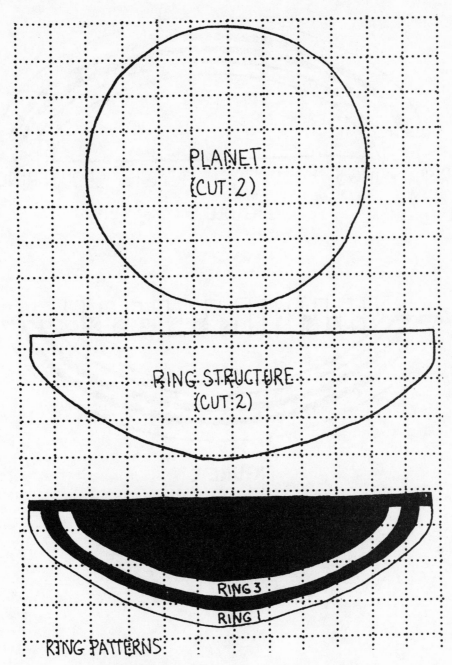

PLANET
(CUT 2)

RING STRUCTURE
(CUT 2)

RING 3

RING 1

RING PATTERNS

FIGURE B (1 sq. = 2½ in.)

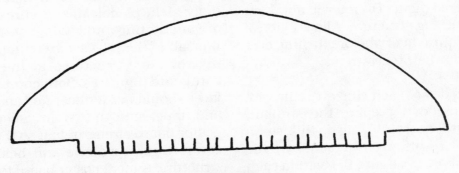

FIGURE C

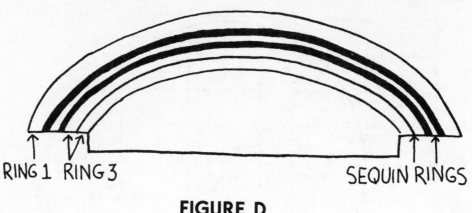

FIGURE D

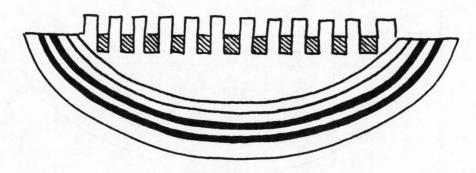

FIGURE E

Repeat the glue and strung-sequin procedure, drawing the line of glue along the center of ring #3 (figure D). You will now have 7 rings on the ring structure. Allow 1 side of the ring structure to dry before turning over and repeating the procedure.

When both sides of each ring structure are completed and dry, prepare the straight, slashed edges for assembly. To do this, simply fold up every other tab (created by the slashes), as shown in figure E. Position each ring structure on the 20-in. corrugated-cardboard circles, so that standing perpendicularly it visually and actually bisects (halves) the planet. Making sure that the tabs are alternating and laying flat on each side, tape all of the tabs securely in place, securing the ring structures to the corrugated cardboard (figure F). Both completed planet faces should be identical. To conceal the tabs and tape, cut the 20-in. sponge-painted poster-board circles in half so that each half covers the area above and below the ring structure. Adhere poster board to corrugated cardboard with staples or double-stick tape.

Hold the planet up to the wearer, aligning the rings at the proper angle (figure A), and mark the position of the shoulders along the inside upper edge. Staple end of each shoulder band to planet at mark. Hold planet up again and staple the remaining band ends to the other planet, aligning the front and back ring structures to create a complete ring (figure G).

ADULT SIZING: No alterations necessary.

SUGGESTIONS: A headband with styrofoam balls attached to represent the moons of Saturn is an amusing touch, as are stickon stars on the face.

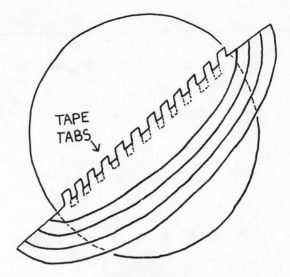

FIGURE F

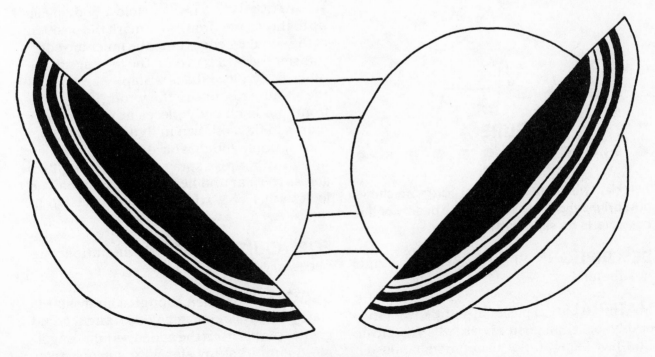

FIGURE G

STAR

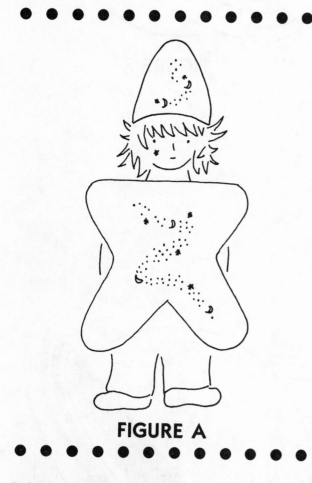

FIGURE A

Twinkle, twinkle little star, this disguise shows how bright and shiny you are. The beauty of this costume is its simplicity.

DESCRIPTION: Shiny slip-on star and headband.

MATERIALS: 3 pieces of shiny silver (preferably) or white poster board; 3½ yds. silver Con-Tact paper, if not using metallic poster board; staples; round-cord elastic; hole punch;

metallic sequins or glitter and glue, plus stick-on stars (optional).

PREPARATIONS: Enlarge the star and headband patterns in figures B and C onto newspaper or brown wrapping paper; cut out. If not using shiny silver poster board, cover 1 side of 3 pieces of poster board with silver Con-Tact paper. Trace headband, 2 star patterns, and two 2-×-12-in. shoulder bands onto poster board; cut out.

TO MAKE HEADBAND: Punch holes near the ends of the headband and tie closed to fit around the head with a piece of round-cord elastic (figure C).

TO MAKE THE STAR: Hold 1 body piece up to the wearer (front) and mark the position of the shoulder edges onto the inner top edge; transfer these marks onto the top edge of the other body piece (back). Staple the ends of the shoulder bands to the wrong side of the front and back body pieces at the shoulder marks to fit, as shown in figure D. For a special, optional touch, star dust can be added by lightly gluing a spray of sequins or glitter across the star and headband. Complete the look with 1 or 2 stick-on stars as shown in figure A.

FOR ADULT SIZING: No alterations are necessary.

SUGGESTIONS: Although a shiny star is featured, any color can be used, and it could get its sparkle from the added sequins or glitter. A simple, shiny star with stick-on stars on the wearer's face is also quite appealing.

162

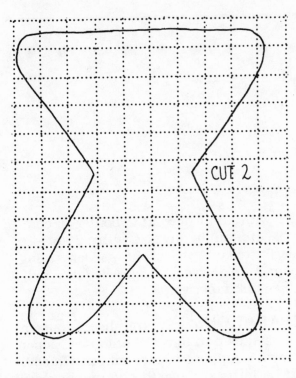

CUT 2

FIGURE B (1 sq. = 2 in.)

FIGURE C (1 sq. = 1½ in.)

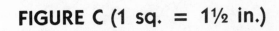

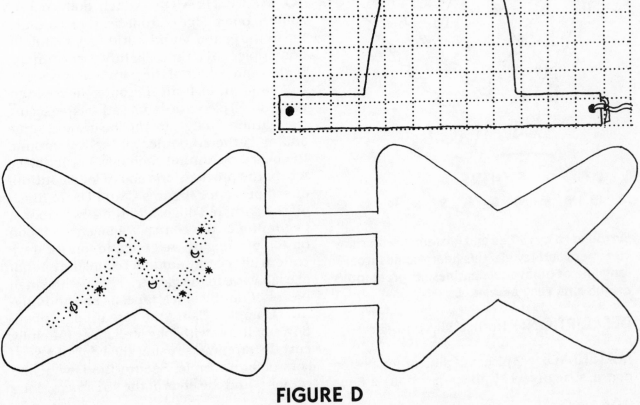

FIGURE D

HEART

FIGURE A

Surrounded by ruffles and glistening with shiny streamers and jewels, this heart comes from a long line of beloved Valentines. Its great looks disguise its easy assembly.

DESCRIPTION: Ruffled slip-on heart.

MATERIALS: 2 pieces of pink or red poster board; 4 or five 14½-in. paper doilies (any shape) with a 3-in. decorative border (or comparable amount in any size with a 2- to 3-in. border); 1 roll or 4 yds. of shiny silver curling ribbon; 2 fake silver 1-in. jewels (optional); double-stick tape; staples.

PREPARATIONS: Enlarge heart pattern piece as shown in figure B onto newspaper or brown wrapping paper; cut out. Trace 2 heart patterns and two 2-×-12-in. shoulder bands (positioned along the top edge) onto pink poster board; cut out. Trim the doily borders from the doilies, cutting ½ in. in from the inner border edge.

TO MAKE HEART: Attach doily border ruffle to outer edge of front heart piece. Starting at the center V and working with 1 doily border piece at a time, slightly gather (inner) undecorated edge of the border and position it ½ to ¾ in. in from the outer heart edge; using small pieces of double-stick tape, secure the gathered edge to the heart. Continue adding gathered border all the way around the heart, beginning each new border piece where the previous one ended for a continuous appearance (figures C and D). To finish off the gathered edge, add the silver ribbon, beginning at the center V. Place the ribbon on top of the gathered edge to form a wave pattern all the way around; secure the bottom of each wave to the gathered edge with small pieces of double-stick tape, as shown in figures C and D. Using the remaining ribbon, tie a small bow with long streamers. Carefully curl the streamers, using the edge of a scissors or blunt knife. Secure the bow at the center V and the ends of the streamers along

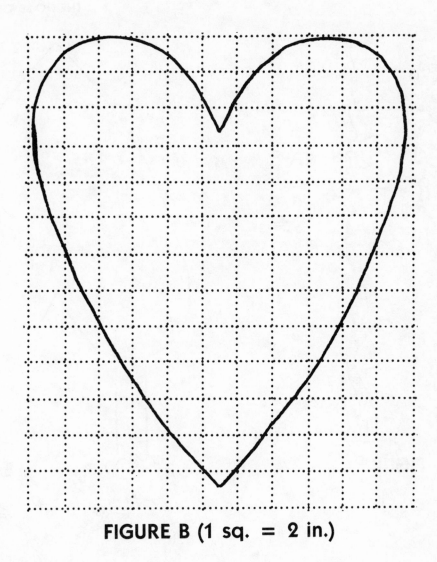

FIGURE B (1 sq. = 2 in.)

the side edges as shown in figure D, using double-stick tape. Add the jewels (optional), using double-stick tape.

To complete the heart, hold the front up to the wearer and mark the position of the shoulder edges onto the inner top edge; transfer these marks onto the top edge of the back heart. Staple the ends of the shoulder bands to the wrong side of the front and back at the shoulder marks to fit, as shown in figure D, concealing the front staples under the ruffle edge.

FOR ADULT SIZING: No alterations are necessary.

SUGGESTIONS: Instead of fake jewels, sequins or glitter can be used for extra sparkle. Decorating the face with small, painted or stick-on hearts adds a bit of whimsical charm to the total look.

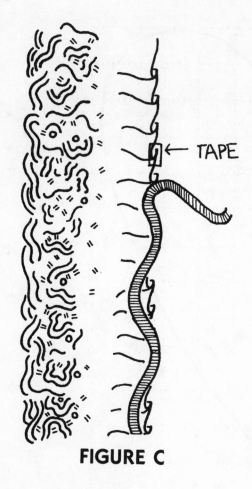

← TAPE

FIGURE C

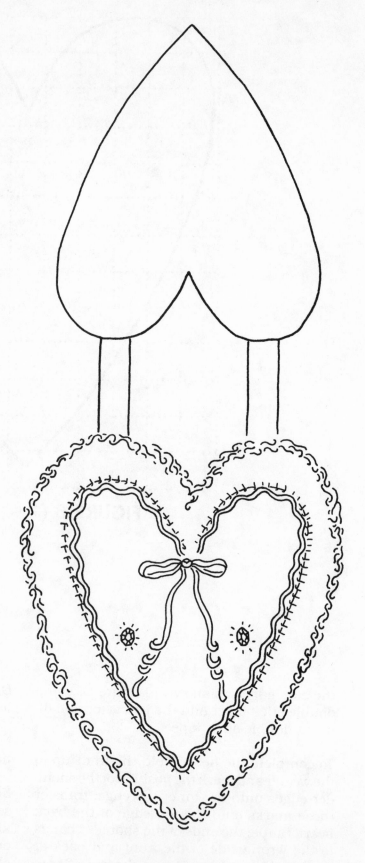

FIGURE D